ROD STRYKER

The
FOUR
DESIRES
WORKBOOK

CREATING A LIFE OF PURPOSE,
HAPPINESS, PROSPERITY,
AND FREEDOM

LIBRARY OF CONGRESS CATALOGUING-IN-PUBLICATION DATA
Stryker, Rod
The Four Desires Workbook/Rod Stryker
Includes bibliographical references.
ISBN 978-1-4951-4904-7 (alk. paper)
1. Yoga 2. Success-Religious aspects-Hinduism. I.Title.
TXu 1-966-314 2015

Printed in the United States of America

Book design by Mary A Wirth

The Four Desires Workbook

Dedicated to Dharma

The mighty purpose woven into the fabric of every soul,
the oceanic intelligence that sustains and guides each of us—and
all of creation—on the path to self-discovery and self-realization.

"There is one thing in this world that you must never forget to do. If you forget
everything else and not this, there's nothing to worry about; but if you remember
everything else and forget this, then you will have done nothing in your life. It's as if a
king has sent you to some country to do a task, and you perform a hundred other
services, but not the one he sent you to do.

So human beings come to this world to do particular work. That work is the purpose,
and each is specific to the person.

Remember the deep root of your being, the presence of your lord. Give your life to the
one who already owns your breath and your moments. If you don't, you will be ...
wasting valuable keenness and foolishly ignoring your dignity and your purpose.

Jalal al-Din Rumi

FOREWORD

It has been nearly four years since my book, The Four Desires: Creating a Life of Purpose, Happiness, Prosperity and Freedom, was published. Not long afterward I found myself having a persistent thought; it would be ideal if there was a workbook to accompany it.

Since the book's release, I have been approached by countless numbers of people wanting to share the powerful and positive impact The Four Desires had on their life. The feedback has been consistent; the book was one of––if not the most––powerfully transformative things they had ever done; it had changed their life. The stories I heard detailed life changing events: achieving otherwise unattainable goals, rediscovering long-lost power, transforming their view of life as a gift––full of possibility, finding a connection to inner wisdom and guidance, in short, they were all about the joy of walking the path to lasting fulfillment.

A common thread links all their stories. In every instance, those who had achieved success had applied the process *fully*––whether with me, at a live workshop or, on their own, with the book. I am touched and gratified to know that the book has helped so many different people achieve so much in the way of enrichment, lasting fulfillment and purposeful living.

When I set out to create The Four Desires, I had no interest in writing just another self-help book. My training in the ancient wisdom of the yoga tradition and my own life-journey ensured that this was not an option. The Four Desires speaks to the greatest of life's undertakings––the achievement of both lasting spiritual and material fulfillment, in other words, true prosperity. Thus, it should come as no surprise, that The Four Desires process can be challenging at times.

This is why I, and all readers of The Four Desires were blessed when Hollace Stephenson, one of my most senior students, took up the task of collating all the exercises in the book and managed to craft the first version of The Four Desires Workbook. After first asking me if it was okay, Hollace–– applying her considerable and intimate working knowledge of the material––created the first draft of the workbook. She then sent it to me, asking for my thoughts and if I would like to proceed. My immediate response was: Yes! Let's proceed and full speed ahead.

Hollace had extracted all the major touch-points of the process from the book, made it spacious and inviting and included useful references from the book as vital background for each of the exercises. She also added some of the new material I've been teaching at live events since the book's release. Her first draft inspired me to write additional content, further refine some of the steps and add my thoughts and personal notes to the reader (see the grey boxes).

The Four Desires Workbook

Nearly two years later, after multiple passes back and forth and with some helpful insights from another senior student and master of the material, Ambika Sue Neufeld, it is ready. I offer my deep gratitude to Hollace for getting this fire started.

I have taken great care to ensure that this workbook incorporates my spirit and tone as a teacher/guide, that the interactive richness that participants experience in live events is woven throughout its pages and that it lights the way to the life I wrote about in The Four Desires.

My recommendation is that you read The Four Desires book first. Then, take up this workbook or if not, if you wish to jump into the process immediately, start with page one of the workbook and have The Four Desires nearby so you can read the sections necessary to complete each of the exercises. Invest yourself totally in the course laid out on these pages; completely dive into each exercise and don't stop. Before you are done you'll find the workbook directing you, one step at a time, to the life your heart longs for you to live (and is prepared to guide you to), the very life you may have been quietly, or not so quietly, dreaming of living.

May The Four Desires Workbook guide and empower all those seeking a more fulfilled life to look within, seek their golden treasure and find eternal fulfillment.

With love,

Yogarupa Rod Stryker

The Four Desires Workbook

Designed to guide you while you complete the process outlined in
The Four Desires: *Creating A Life Of Purpose, Happiness, Prosperity, And Freedom*
Written By Rod Stryker

Table of Contents

All of the exercises in this workbook are designed to guide you through the process of *The Four Desires*. Do your best to complete them all. There are some specific exercises that are critical landmarks and must be completed in order to truly engage the full power of the process, and thus fully propel you to lasting freedom and fulfillment. These key exercises are **bolded** below.

INTRODUCTION

"Learn to hear destiny's call and to answer it with your best life." – Rod Stryker

In 2009, I took Rod Stryker's course based on *The Four Desires* process. It made a significant impact on how I live my life; with more purpose and self-inquiry than I ever had. Through the process, he gave me profound self-inquiry tools to continue moving closer and closer each year to my very best life. When *The Four Desires* was published, I read it and completed the exercises on my own. Again, I examined my habits and thoughts and made more strides toward an even fuller life as I came back to refine each of my statements and get clear on how I align my actions with my life's purpose. I keep *The Four Desires* handy and redo the exercises often; the process has become a profound influence in my life.

Because the work in his book can be daunting without guidance or motivation, I felt compelled to help Rod create a way to help others complete the process when they couldn't get to a Four Desires workshop. Having a background in science education and skill in developing scaffolding for students to work through challenges, as well as having gone through the process several times with Rod's guidance and on my own, I felt I had the experience to help him create a workbook for *The Four Desires* and the first drafts of this workbook were born.

This workbook is intended to make it easy for you to complete the process detailed in *The Four Desires* and ensure that you are successful in achieving the book's aim. Since the book was published, Rod has further developed *The Four Desires* process and this workbook to help you discover the essential knowledge that leads to a life of true wisdom and ultimate fulfillment. The exercises and questions you will do are based on the *Vedas*, the ancient spiritual tradition that is the source of yoga. The basis of this process is *vichara,* the profound practice of finding clarity around life's most essential questions.

As a student, teacher, and practitioner of ParaYoga, I have learned that the way to true fulfillment is through self-inquiry and consistent, steady practice. Through those efforts we realize our soul's purpose, recognize our true potential and are empowered to take the actions that bring lasting fulfillment.

To my Teacher, Yogarupa Rod Stryker, thank you for giving me the tools to live a fulfilled and purposeful life in a language I understand. Thank you also for your confidence in my abilities to help you create this workbook and share the process with others. May it be a way to spread the teachings and to support all that read your book, *The Four Desires*.

In Gratitude,
Hollace Stephenson
Certified ParaYoga Level I

How To Use This Workbook

To get maximum benefit, you will need to do all of the exercises here; this is a systematic process. This workbook facilitates the most vital and precious work from *The Four Desires*, inspiring and guiding you to complete each exercise and providing you with the support to discover and then navigate your soul's unique path. This workbook is intended to ensure that all who read *The Four Desires* achieve their four desires. This process can be done over and over again and, you are encouraged to do so.

As you read *The Four Desires*, Rod explains and details each exercise to you. Use this workbook as your playground of discovery and self-exploration. Here, you will read introductions to each exercise follow step by step instructions and find space to work through the entire process including several new exercises and steps developed since *The Four Desires* was published. With the aid of the workbook simplifying each step, guiding and inspiring you along the way, dive deep to uncover the powerful and transformative wisdom that resides within you. Soon, with the aid of this workbook, you will find yourself forging ahead and gaining momentum toward finding the meaning and purpose of your life. You are encouraged to draft, write, scribble, add images, and more blank pages, draw pictures and do whatever it takes to complete the exercises. Move through each one courageously; when you feel challenged, keep going. The only way out of resistance is to—sooner or later—move through it. So, why put off your happiness? Move through the workbook steadily--yes, by doing so you will engage a consistent and steady practice that will lead to "true fulfillment."

Once you complete this workbook the first time, you'll be able to look back at how much you progressed and just how much your efforts have helped add to the miracle that is you and your life. Come back to your writings here, and feel free to continue exploring. Redo the exercises when you need to and watch as you achieve your desires. Your first time completing this work won't be the last. Do the exercises in the book anytime you seek fulfillment.

"You are the architect of your life and you decide your destiny," said Swami Rama. Make up your mind to achieve and you will, but not by wishing alone. Only by taking the necessary actions toward your own fulfillment and reducing internal resistance to change will you realize the potential of your own power.

> *Welcome to the first step in the process of tapping into your soul's guiding intelligence to create a life of purpose, happiness, prosperity and freedom! Before you begin reading and writing, I am going to ask you to take a few moments to experience your own unique sense of what it feels like to thrive. You will start by recalling the joy and the deep satisfaction of total fulfillment. Whether this sounds easy or hard, it's essential you start with this step, and thus light the very spark that inspires all of us to seek and achieve fulfillment.*

Overview of the practice:

To prepare for this contemplation, you will meditate on your breath. First, you'll establish a comfortable, seated position with your spine tall (use a chair if you prefer).

Next, you'll close your eyes and become aware of your breath, watching it move in and out of your nostrils for a few minutes. You'll just focus on your breath, while becoming more and more effortless. You'll observe the air moving through your nostrils, continuing until you perceive your mind becoming quiet. This may take a few minutes. Don't worry if you are distracted; just keep returning to your breath. Don't rush. Just be as effortless as possible, completely relax; just follow your breath. You'll continue, until you perceive a "presence" behind your thoughts—a presence of simple awareness.

Once your mind is quiet… you'll recall a time in your life when you felt fully alive, a time when you experienced your very best self, being fully present. Immerse yourself in the experience of thriving by evoking a time when you were an unstoppable force. This does not necessarily mean that you choose to remember a time when everything was "perfect"—it's ideal that you recall a time when you were thriving **in spite of (or despite) your circumstances, not because of your circumstances.** In other words, remember a time in your life when you were fully alive, flourishing **despite being challenged.**

For a few minutes you will let your mind and body be saturated in the remembrance of this most special time in your life. Just rest in it. Soak it up. Feel the feelings, witness the thoughts, and absorb all of it, mentally, emotionally and even physically. Make it a living reality now. For these few minutes experience as much as you can about this moment of truly and completely thriving!

Set a timer for 5-10 minutes. Practice the breath meditation, followed by contemplating and resting in this Thriving Moment.

Next, without giving it any thought or judgment, you'll take 5 minutes to write a free-form poem about this moment. Yes, a poem! Think of your thriving moment; think of the deep joy, satisfaction and meaning of moving through challenges and realizing your potential. Write about how you got through it. How you embodied it. What it felt and looked like. Be spontaneous and allow the poem (which does not have to rhyme or fit any form) to flow through you. The truth about this auspicious experience is in you. Use the space provided on the next page to give it form and make it real.

A note about writing your poem: Most times that I ask a group to write a poem, there's a collective sigh in the room. Few of us write poetry, including the idea that we are not eloquent enough, nor possess the skill to write anything worthy of being called a poem. In my experience, the opposite is true. Rarely have I seen a poem written in one of my workshops where I (and the attendees) am not blown away by their depth and originality. Don't worry about the outcome, just express what you felt and saw. Your authentic voice of wisdom is already a part of you; it may have been waiting for this opportunity to share its insights with you. Given a chance, it will and is sure to surprise you with some of what it knows. So, go ahead and start: meditate on your breath, followed by absorption in a complete sense of thriving and finally, write your poem.

Time: 10-15 minutes

Step 1. Sit in a comfortable seated position

Step 2. Meditate on the flow of your breath

Step 3. Once your mind gets calm, settle into the experience of effortless awareness

Step 4. Begin to recall your Thriving Moment. Contemplate the moment in great detail, making it fully alive. Experience all the sights, feelings and thoughts that arise from you being completely immersed in this moment, sense all of the victorious satisfaction of **moving through the challenges that led you to this unique and awe-inspiring moment.**

Step 5. After meditation and visualization, take 5 minutes and use the space on the following page to write a poem about it. You are not confined to any particular form. Please be creative, spontaneous and allow your Thriving Moment to flow through you. Describe every feeling you experience, write about overcoming the challenges, write about the victory, the redemption of it all — write about being fully and uniquely you.

"The foundation for lasting happiness and fulfillment is finding and living your life's purpose." – Rod Stryker

Read chapters 1-5 in *The Four Desires* to clearly understand the principles of lasting fulfillment, the four types of desire and the critical piece of finding your mighty purpose and writing it as an empowering statement called your Dharma Code (DC). Before you begin this process, please be patient and give yourself time to read thoroughly.

❖ **Pages 20-23** describe the four desires that are the undercurrent that compel you toward achieving your unique and highest destiny.

❖ On **pages 36-43** there are important points regarding *dharma*. In this section of *The Four Desires* process you will focus on uncovering your unique *dharma* and creating it as a clear and evocative statement(s).

❖ On **page 39 read Laura's story** about how acting on her DC established a path for her to achieve the lasting happiness and fulfillment she deeply desired.

❖ On **pages 51-67** is a complete explanation for creating a DC. To help you uncover your soul's unique blueprint for happiness—your DC, you will first complete several journal exercises.

When you're done reading, return to this page in the workbook and go through each step. Here you will find some extra and important hints about how to create *your* DC.

Step 1. Imagining a Life Well Lived: Your Own. See yourself celebrating a significant birthday sometime near the end of your life after having achieved a life of ultimate fulfillment, success and meaning in all four desires. Next, imagine that your closest friends, family, loved ones and associates from every walk of your life gather to pay tribute to you having lived your best life. What will your life look like? One way to answer this question is to consider the result of having lived the next fifty years, completely committed to living from the vision and passion described in your poem. What if from this moment forward you live mightily and invest all of yourself purposefully toward the fulfillment of all four of your desires? This exercise entails you writing from the perspective of four people, each of whom will stand and speak about you, the unique outcomes of you having lived your very best life, and the challenges and accomplishments of your life. If you feel you need more information, please go to page 51-67 in *The Four Desires* for complete instructions and examples of testimonials.

Under each category on the next page, list five to ten people who come to mind whom you love and respect. List people that you feel know you, your hopes and dreams, your inner truths and outer accomplishments within that category of desire. You can list people who are no longer alive even if you didn't know them, as long as they are or have been a real person—no imaginary friends please—and you genuinely feel as though you could speak through them. For example, you could list a world leader you may admire and relate to, a deceased relative or friend who you feel confident that you can speak/write from their perspective. Get past your rational mind and just start writing names of people until you are done with each list. You can list any name more than once, in as many or as few of the categories as you like.

> *If you are tempted to stop here, to close the workbook and do something else—don't. You are worth the investment of your time and energy to keep moving forward. If you don't follow through, there's a good chance the very things about your life that you wish were different, will remain the same. Moreover, there's a good chance you will continue to act without the benefit of knowing if all of your efforts are consistent with the deeper meaning and purpose of your life. So, forge ahead. This exercise is the foundation for much more to come and, often times is a source of joyful discovery and empowerment.*

Time: 5 minutes

List five to ten people who come to mind under each category. You can list any name more than once, in as many or as few of the categories as you like. Don't over-think this; just start writing names.

Dharma	Artha	Kama	Moksha

Step 2. The Tribute—Look at your lists of names under each desire and circle the one person you would most like to hear speak about your life in that category of desire. Pick a different person to speak about you in each category of desire. In other words, you will be writing four different testimonials, each one from the viewpoint of a different person. One person per category of desire, please.

> *You might be wondering, "Why? Why write in someone else's voice?" The answer is simple: people who know and care about you are able to see you in ways that often times you are unable to recognize. The result of completing all the steps in this exercise will expand your self-understanding and help you to claim a more complete vision of who you are and who you can become. Yes, it will take up to an hour to complete, but when you are done, you will have opened your mind and heart to so many possibilities.*

Time: 1 hour

Once you've circled one name for each category, start the process of writing your testimonials. On the next several pages, write the name of the person you chose in each category. Once you put pen to paper, keep writing continuously for 10-15 minutes. Consider the tips below to write from a completely free, non-judgmental place.

<u>**Helpful Tips:**</u>

- ❖ **Envision the end of your life, having lived the next fifty years as the unstoppable, thriving being described in your poem. Imagine that you acted consistently, completely aligned with your best, most powerful self. Write about the results of where you wound up.**

- ❖ **Use your imagination, but be authentic. Your testimonials should describe the ultimate you and your accomplishments, but they also need to be practical.**

- ❖ **Be spontaneous and intuitive as you write, don't struggle with your rational mind. Please don't worry about complete sentences, sentence structure, grammar or spelling. Don't judge, over-think or censor what comes to your consciousness at all.**

- ❖ **List specific accomplishments, things you overcame to be successful, your life philosophy, and relationships, things of which you are most proud; include as many specific details as possible.**

- ❖ **Keep the details in each testimonial consistent with the specific desire you are writing about.**

- ❖ **If words or phrases come to mind that make no sense to you, write them anyway.**

- ❖ **Write as fast as you can. Once you put pen to paper don't stop until you're done with the testimonial in that particular voice addressing that particular desire. Write as a continuous flow/stream of consciousness.**

Time: 15 minutes

Desire: *dharma*

Speaker: _____

Desire: *dharma* continued…

Time: 15 minutes

Desire: *artha*

Speaker: _____

Desire: *artha* continued…

Time: 15 minutes

Desire: *kama*

Speaker: _____

Desire: *kama* continued…

Time: 15 minutes

Desire: *moksha*

Speaker: _____

Desire: *moksha* continued…

Step 3: Identify key words and phrases from your testimonials

A. Read through your testimonials and highlight key words and phrases that are the most compelling and significant; the ones that express the key ideas and relevant themes of your life and that speak to the core of who you are.

B. Once you have highlighted your key words and phrases for all four testimonials, take some time and reflect on them. These are the values and priorities that will lead you to and keep you on the path to a fulfilled life. As you reflect, think about how closely your present life is in harmony with the words and phrases.

C. Pare down your list of key words and phrases. Circle only the ones that are the most compelling, energizing or perhaps unnerving. Circle the highlights that jump out, that express vital underlying themes, convey ideas or feelings that you genuinely aspire to, or encapsulate the challenges you have overcome in your past.

D. Read over your circled, highlighted words and step into the ideas and most vital points they reveal. Be aware of how your body responds, and feelings that arise.

E. You will pare down the list one more time. Write down every key word and phrase that feels essential, and that could inform your DC. Keep in mind, it is not mandatory that any of these words appear in your DC. These words or phrases are meant to stimulate ideas and move you toward discovery. Your DC may (or may not) include any of this collection of ideas, but there is a good chance that one or two nuggets will be part of your DC. Don't prejudge which ones will be. At this point, your job is just to gather the vital clues for your finished DC.

Write all of the essential key words & phrases from your testimonials here:

!Before continuing with the Dharma Code Exercise, please do the meditation on the following page. This vital practice is called An Experiment in Watching Your Mind Think. After doing the meditation, you'll move on to two journal exercises that are designed to help you gather even more clues to uncover your DC. *I use both of them at live trainings of The Four Desires.*

"Your mind has measureless capacity to affect the quality and content of your life." – Rod Stryker

A distracted or turbulent mind is unable to perceive the soul or the subtle guidance of *dharma*. If you are to be able to access this kind of higher intelligence, you must first learn to focus and then develop deeper awareness. It all comes down to this: your soul is ever-present, always ready to guide you. However, your mind's potential to perceive the gifts of your soul and the guiding influence of your *dharma* must be cultivated.

This exercise will help show you why it requires effort to find and live your *dharma*. It will also begin to awaken the mind's higher potentials.

Time: 2 minutes
Find a comfortable seated position. Close your eyes, still your body and for two minutes observe your thoughts. For 120 seconds, count each time you have a thought. You can use a timer so you won't have to think about the time.

I know, I know. This seems like an inconsequential exercise, a step you could skip. But, please consider this: the very first benefit of facing your mind's "distractedness" is a greater sense of self-acceptance, not to mention insight. Indeed, once you've experienced how fleeting the present moment is and how much, or how little, your mind actually spends in the present, you are likely to have a much clearer understanding of why you are not as fulfilled as you would hope to be, or that you struggle for solutions to your challenges. Each and every time you actually observe your mind—and thus, be more present, whenever you can become aware of the countless moments when you are not present—you will gain clarity about who you are and what you can do to have more of what you really want.

All you're going to do is observe your mind thinking for two minutes. Ready. Set. Go.

Two minutes later…

❖ **How many thoughts did you have?**

❖ **Did you stop counting before the two minutes were up?**

!Read the information in the gray box on pages 70-71 in *The Four Desires* to learn about the effects multitasking has on your brain versus the effects of meditation.

The Four Desires Workbook

"Imagine being able, at any time, to experience the joy of having fulfilled your every desire. That is exactly what is possible when you simply learn to still your mind." – Rod Stryker

Take a few minutes to steady your thoughts, to see the beauty and wisdom that lies beyond them. You can read instructions beginning on page 72 in *The Four Desires* and the companion CD contains an introduction and guided practice. Please practice this often, ideally on a daily basis. Keep a log here whenever you do this meditation.

Date	Duration	Reflection

"When dharma informs your decisions, you align yourself with the power that moves the world."
– Rod Stryker

This exercise is another invaluable step to gather even more clues about your soul's unique purpose—your authentic DC. It will ask you to intuitively uncover three key words that capture the essence of who and what you are. Again, you will be best served if you avoid trying to intellectually come up with the three words. This is why you will use meditation to still your mind before trying to determine your three words. Once your intellect is still, you will pose the question to your higher self: "Who am I?" If you are indeed still, you will perceive a subtle, but definitive response. Trust what you hear, especially if the answer(s) seem to have come from a decisive and unequivocal source, deep within. In that case, your three words will be unique and authentic. You will repeat the question until you have heard three words.

Use this exercise, Three Words, to identify three terms that identify the deepest part of you.

Time: 25 minutes (Please read all instructions below before you begin practice.)

- ❖ You'll be listening to a guided meditation from the *The Four Desires* companion CD in preparation for this exercise so, please set up your iPod, computer or MP3 player in a comfortable environment.

- ❖ Find a comfortable seated position to practice the Meditation to Increase the Power of Soul.

- ❖ After the guided meditation, allow your thoughts to remain still and tune to a sense of pure intelligence.

- ❖ As you allow yourself to relax and rest in silent awareness, ask this infinite intelligence the following question, "Who am I?"

- ❖ Then, simply listen. Ask again and again, constantly remembering the feeling of silence in between each time

> *It's likely you will experience a sense of calm and certainty as these three words are revealed, having sensed that they have arisen from a deep quality of "knowing." It's also likely that one of three words will surprise you and, perhaps, not make complete sense. This a good sign.*

you pose the question. Eventually you will "hear" three words that describe your true essence. Don't try or struggle with this. Just relax and listen, simply allow the three words to be revealed. At least one if not all three should surprise you.

- ❖ As soon as they do, use the spaces provided below to write down your three words.

1. **Practice the Meditation to Increase the Power of Soul from the companion CD.**

2. **Ask yourself, "Who am I?" again and again until you have your three words.**

3. **At least one, if not all three words should surprise you!**

4. **Use the space provided below to write three words that surface:**

_____ _____ _____

"Man has come into this world for a particular task, and that is his purpose;
if he does not perform it, then he will have done nothing." – Rumi

Have you ever found yourself repeatedly facing the same life lesson(s) over and over again? Replicating both positive and negative patterns? Have you watched yourself attract, or even create, similar dynamics in your relationships, some fulfilling and some unfulfilling? What recurring themes have been a consistent part of your life?

Indeed, we all have patterns, good and bad, constructive as well as destructive. It can feel as though these patterns are literally part of us, given the fact that they often exert themselves more forcefully than our intention to avoid them. Indeed, these deep-seated patterns are part of the unconscious fabric that determines our motivations and desires—the very stuff that either obstructs us from (or facilitates us) realizing ultimate freedom and fulfillment.

It is vital that you take both positive and "negative" themes into account in the process of shaping your DC. I suggest that if you recognize two strong helpful themes/patterns, you add at least one theme that is not positive or, if you find two powerful challenging themes, include at least one that is positive/empowering.

Indeed, learning to acknowledge and overcome your patterns—constructive as well as non-constructive—plays a vital role in you fulfilling your destiny.

Here are examples of patterns/themes from others who have taken *The Four Desires* Workshop:

- ❖ I avoid taking risks
- ❖ Inadequacy
- ❖ I am constantly pulled away from what I know is important
- ❖ I'll sacrifice everything for success
- ❖ To stay healthy is a constant struggle

- ❖ Overwork
- ❖ Relentlessly driven to succeed
- ❖ Procrastination
- ❖ I am resilient through change
- ❖ I see multiple perspectives
- ❖ I feel unheard/unseen
- ❖ I manifest goals with ease

On the next page please write down 3-5 recurrent **themes in your life**. The intention of this exercise is to help you specify the patterns, habitual life lessons, **both positive and negative**, that have reoccurred throughout your life—over and over again.

> *Take your time with this exercise. You may want to start by jotting down a few ideas. Then, take a walk, a shower, or a hike. Clear your mind and consider the patterns you have dealt with over the years. It often helps to step away from concerted effort; instead give yourself space to find the words that describe the binding patterns you have experienced for years, or even decades. This is not as hard as it might sound. You are looking to acknowledge your all-too-familiar patterns. It's safe to say that the correct answers to this exercise will be things that you have recognized many times in the past.*

Time: 15 minutes or as much time as you need.

- ❖ **What situations do you repeatedly find yourself experiencing?**
- ❖ **What engrained patterns of behavior and mechanical ways do you have of responding to situations?**
- ❖ **What conditions, feelings, or circumstances do you find being recycled over and over again?**
- ❖ **What is the universe constantly trying to tell you, and/or what conditions keep presenting themselves?**

Before you begin to draft the first version of your DC, use this page to compile the clues you've uncovered. Please collect the most essential or evocative (perhaps unnerving) phrases and words you have written in the last four journal exercises and write them in their corresponding spaces below.

Poem Highlights (pg. 5)	Testimonials Key Words & Phrases (pg. 17 & 18)
Three Words (pg. 21)	**Themes (pg. 23 & 24)**

! *It's highly likely that there are phrases, words or ideas from any or all of these boxes that will either be central to or a part of your final DC.*

Your DC will evolve over time. It will be refined as you become more clear and insightful about your soul's purpose. Future exercises will help shed more light on how your DC needs to change to convey the totality of your soul's purpose. For the time being, the process begins here. Be creative and have fun. After all, this is your first pass at creating your DC.

To arrive at your authentic DC, it is essential you have completed all of the previous work. Be sure you have worked through all of the workbook exercises so far:

> *Trust me, you will likely write several drafts before you arrive at your final and fully developed DC. YOUR FIRST ONE DOES NOT HAVE TO BE PERFECT.*

- ❖ The Thriving Moment poem
- ❖ Your testimonials
- ❖ Three Words that describe you
- ❖ Themes in Your Life

Once you have completed all the exercises, you have everything you need to craft the first draft of your DC. Distilling the content from your grid, your mission is to create clear and precise language that describes exactly how you would wish (and need) to respond to every moment in your life and ultimately, achieve the life you described in your testimonials. Your DC, must be a powerful statement(s) that speaks to all four desires; it must be able to direct you to overcome all obstacles/patterns and is your call to action toward fulfilling a life of purpose, prosperity, happiness and freedom. It will honor the big *Dharma* (universal) as well as the small *dharma* (personal). It's not important for others to know what your DC means. It is imperative that it is invocative and provocative to you.

!Recall Laura's Story and the essential lesson for anyone wanting a truly fulfilled life on pages 39-43 of *The Four Desires.*

Dharma Code Guidelines:

- ❖ Your DC has been a part of you all along
- ❖ It will need to be strong and compelling enough to move you through the doubt, fear and obstacles that you will inevitably encounter on the way to becoming your best self
- ❖ It must inspire and animate you to fulfill all four of your desires
- ❖ It must exemplify a clear way of responding to every moment
- ❖ Ask yourself the following question, "Will my DC lead me to the ideal life outlined in my testimonials?"

A Powerful Dharma Code Must:

- ❖ Be worded in clear, practical terms
- ❖ Be a call to action
- ❖ Be a source of guidance when you feel lost or have to choose among conflicting desires
- ❖ Guide you to meet the challenges to achieve your ideal life as described in your testimonials

Helpful Tips:

- ❖ Word it clearly, in a way that is profound to you
- ❖ Write your DC in present tense, rather than future tense
- ❖ Emphasize verbs in their active form as opposed to verbs in their passive form that end in "ing."

Considering all of the above, I strongly suggest you don't try to forge all of the essential elements of your DC into one sentence. Rarely have I seen a single sentence accomplish all that a DC must encapsulate. Take for example what we could consider to be Mahatma Gandhi's DC, below. Clearly one sentence would not have helped set in motion all that he was striving to accomplish.

> *"Let the first act of every morning be to make the following resolves for the day:*
> *I shall not fear anyone on Earth, I shall fear only God.*
> *I shall not bear ill toward anyone.*
> *I shall not submit to injustice from anyone.*
> *I shall conquer untruth by truth, and in resisting untruth, I shall put up with all suffering."*
> *-- Mahatma Gandhi*

*You may also find 2 to 4 sentences is what your DC will require to be complete. Also, I don't suggest using statements that begin with, "I am..." For example, "I am luminous fire" or "I am the dance of divinity." (Don't be concerned if you would have never thought to use terms like these). The simple fact is that sooner or later, life will provide evidence that you are not "luminous fire," or "the dance of divinity." Keep your statement(s) active. Less declarative, like "I am," and more toward what you **can and will do**, like "I shall conquer untruth by truth..."*

Review Appendix A at the back of this workbook to read examples of DCs. **It's important to note that <u>none of those examples are your DC</u>**. Although you may be inspired by any one of them, remember: yours will be unique and original. The samples are for reference only, you'll still need to create your own, by taking account of the full measure of who you are as revealed by the exercises listed above.

Before writing, here are my final suggestions on creating your first DC draft:

1) *Don't start from scratch. There's a good chance that there is at least one phrase in your poem that needs to be in your DC or, for that matter, consider making at least one of your themes or one of your three words, from the "who am I?" exercise, as a central part of your DC. In each case, consider the terms or ideas that are the most original, most powerful—that somehow, just stand out—you are original, so what defines you must also be original.*

2) *DC is a big idea! Don't stop developing it until you are certain that your DC covers the full range of your four desires.*

3) ***Avoid the all too common desire to make your DC all about serving others.*** *I can't tell you how many DCs start out being all about "serving," all about "following the light," "serving God," "being a vehicle for love and divinity." Of course these are wonderful sentiments, but the reality is that, if your DC fails to empower you, it won't work. It is true that there is a "Universal Dharma Code," that goes something like: **"To love, serve and give."** However, if you focus on that, above all else, you may find yourself repeating some of your most unproductive patterns. On the other hand, if your Code elucidates your unique way of serving your highest self-interest and you intersperse it with the very things that bring you joy and keep you on the path of thriving—recall your poem and the gold nuggets from your testimonials—you will have a code that uplifts all and everything. Thus, Your DC can include a maximum of one of those words (love, serve or give) but **not** all three or even two. **Love, serve or give—only one can be in your DC.***

4) *One last thing, please remember that your DC must be powerful enough to not only motivate you to thrive, but moreover to get you through those dark moments in life when you are confused, challenged, discouraged or alone. More than likely, your DC will include some of what you acknowledged as the themes/core patterns in your life—positive or negative.*

Dharma Code Initial Ideas:

Use this page to jot down ideas for first drafts of your DC.

Refine it. Write your first powerful version of a Dharma Code:

_____

_____

_____

_____

_____

Take a few moments to reflect on what you have written. Read it out loud. What is missing that needs to be in your DC? Re-write the version your best friend would be thrilled to read.

_____

_____

_____

_____

_____

One last time, is there a vital nugget from your grid that needs to be added? Another sentence? Write your finished first draft.

_____

_____

_____

_____

_____

Step 4: Share Your Dharma Code

Once you have a draft of your DC, find someone you can share it with. This can be anyone that you trust will give you feedback in a supportive way. Reading it out loud can be a powerful tool for arriving at your final DC. Find someone who is like-minded and can embrace, not be threatened by, your enthusiasm and commitment to change for the better.

"The vows we make, whether constructive or destructive, whether made consciously or unconsciously are the forces that create our world, our destiny." – Rod Stryker

After reading Chapter 10 in *The Four Desires*, come back to this workbook and complete pages 32-34, the beginning of The Sankalpa Exercise. A *sankalpa* is a vow, a resolve that you do everything in your capacity to achieve or become. For our purposes it will be something you intend to accomplish in the next 6-18 months. **The following is a systematic 7-step process that ensures you will write an effective *sankalpa*.** Please skim through the entire process listed here before beginning Step 1 on the next page; this will help you develop an understanding of how each step builds upon the previous.

7 Steps of Sankalpa	Book Reference	Workbook Reference
Step 1: Review the four desires	Page 98	Page 32
Step 2: Practice The Bliss Meditation	Page 99 & companion CD	Page 33
Steps 3: Access the wisdom of your soul	Page 101	Page 33
Step 4: Allow your higher self to identify which desire you need to fulfill	Page 101	Page 33-34
Pause the Sankalpa Exercise to identify your *vikalpa*	Page 146	Page 35-46
Then, Second Draft of Your Dharma Code		Page 47-53
Step 5: Create a Mind Map of the ways fulfilling your desire will positively affect your life	Page 102	Page 54
Step 6: Specify the goal your soul is prompting you to achieve	Page 104	Page 55-56
Workbook Bonus: Create Your Vision		Page 57-58
Step 7: 1st Draft of Your *Sankalpa*	Page 106	Page 59-60
Sankalpa 2.0		Page 61

!Read. The truth is we all know what we want, but we don't always know what we need. A powerful example of this can be found in Victoria's Story on pages 88-90 in *The Four Desires.*

"The masterpiece of man, is to live to the purpose." – Benjamin Franklin

Step 1. Review the four desires. Read the short descriptions of the four desires below to become more familiar with them. Keep this list close by when you complete Step 2; you will need it so that you can open your eyes after the meditation and immediately refer to it. As you read through this list, don't try to figure out anything ahead of time nor anticipate which one of the four desires your soul might point you toward fulfilling.

Dharma is the longing for purpose, the drive to become who you are meant to be. This is the longing to fulfill your potential and contribute to the world. *Dharma* is based on the understanding that the world and all beings in it are linked. Thus, *dharma* is the longing to support the larger good—to give more than you take. *Dharma* focuses on how you embody virtue in your day-to-day life, your career, as well as your other roles in the world, provided that they contribute to something greater than your personal needs. *Dharma* can include your job or being a full-time mom, environmentalist, Scout leader or PTA volunteer. The aim of *dharma* is for a life that is balanced and sustainable and that positively fulfills the deeper meaning and purpose of your life. It is the drive for selflessness, charity and being a living example to yourself and others of what you truly aspire to be and become.

Artha is the longing for the means you require to fulfill your *dharma* and to tend to your other desires. It includes the desire for financial and material security, physical well-being, and a stable, secure home. It also includes any other things you require that support you in the pursuit of your higher ideals and goals.

Kama is the longing for pleasure: Sensual and sexual pleasure, friendship, intimacy, family, beauty, art, fellowship, play, adventure, creativity and joy. It also includes the desire for the pleasure that accompanies ambitions fulfilled (all things first aspired to and then achieved produce a feeling of pleasure).

Moksha is the longing for true freedom and spiritual awareness. This means being able to live fully, unburdened by your life and the things in it. Moksha is the intrinsic desire to realize a state beyond the confines of the other three desires. It is the longing to move beyond all suffering and fear and realize the highest of all joys. It is the hunger to know and merge with the highest Truth, Essence, or Creator. It is the basis for humanity seeking prayer, meditation, contemplation, self-reflection and deep self-inquiry.

The Bliss Meditation will prepare you to identify the unique desire that your soul is pointing you toward achieving––and thus, open the door to creating your *sankalpa* from an absolutely intuitive place. You can read instructions for these steps on page 99 in *The Four Desires*. The companion CD contains an introduction and guided practice to The Bliss Meditation. You can practice as often as you'd like to touch real and lasting joy and deep, deep contentment.

Please read all the steps below before you begin practice.

Step 2. **Practice The Bliss Meditation.** First, listen to the Introduction to The Bliss Meditation on *The Four Desires* companion CD and read step 3. Then, practice the meditation. Have this workbook open to page 32, or the book open to page 98, so you can refer to the four desires when you get to step 4. Keep your eyes closed throughout the meditation and step 3.

Step 3. Access the wisdom of your soul. Once you have completed The Bliss Meditation, keep your eyes closed and tune to your wisdom center, the place of knowingness within you. It could be your gut, for some it's the heart, for others it might be the third eye center. The important thing is to rest in a deep state of contentment, then settle and finally, turn inward to the feeling of knowingness and certainty within you. Feel connected to the inner core of truth that is always ready and fully capable of guiding you to your best life, the part of you that knows exactly what you need and what you don't need.

Step 4. Allow your higher self to identify the desire that it would have you fulfill. Open your eyes, continue to rest in contentment and ask your higher self the following question: "Which one of the four desires, if it was fulfilled in the next six to eighteen months, would best serve my highest purpose or *dharma*?" Allow your inner voice to provide the answer. Don't let your rational mind take over this process; it must be organic and intuitive. If you don't feel a clear definitive answer, or if you are less than clear, close your eyes and repeat steps 2 & 3.

When you open your eyes, softly look at the grid below and circle which of the four desires you are called to fulfill by your highest self. Please rest your intellect, don't allow it to choose, circle the one that you are organically and intuitively drawn to.

Moksha	Kama
Artha	Dharma

In the middle of the oval below, write the name of the category of desire that your higher self just identified in your meditation.

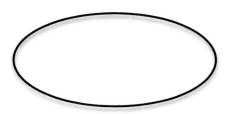

! Now, take a break and absorb the work you've done so far. **Before you go any further with your *sankalpa* and ultimately fulfill your resolve, you'll do some pivotal work to find out what is keeping you from greatness.**

> *What follows may be the most vital exercise in the entire process of The Four Desires—perhaps the one, more than any other—that will ensure a life of fulfillment and purpose.*

"If you want to identify me, ask me not where I live, or what I like to eat or how I comb my hair, but ask me what I think I am living for, in detail, and ask me what I think is keeping me from living fully for the thing I want to live for. Between these two answers you can determine the identity of any person." **– Thomas Merton**

!Read Evan's Story beginning on page 142 in *The Four Desires*, it is a chilling reminder of just how destructive a *vikalpa* can be and how unearthing it can free and empower you to fulfill your own heart's desires.

!Read Go to page 140 in *The Four Desires* and read A Fork in the Wishing Road. After you've read it, come back to the workbook and begin the process of identifying the resistance, moreover, the desire that has kept you from fulfilling the similar intentions as those outlined in your mind map and, in a far more all-encompassing way, your *dharma*.

Time: 20-25 minutes
In this 5-step exercise, you are going to be your own best friend, therapist and spiritual guide.

> *You're going to identify the resistance—moreover, the desire at the root of your pattern—the one that stands in the way of you fulfilling your specific intention and, more than likely, much, much more. This type of desire is known as a vikalpa, a desire that creates resistance and is in conflict with you fulfilling your soul's purpose. Most of us can acknowledge that we are at times our own biggest obstacle, the greatest resistance to achieving our goals. However, in this exercise you are going to go one very critical step further. You are going to recognize and thereby acknowledge the resistance, not just by identifying it, but rather specifying what it is you want that is the source of your resistance. Yes, the critical step in this exercise is to acknowledge what you get out of perpetuating the pattern that keeps you from fulfilling your higher purpose and goal(s). In other words, your resistance is rooted in a desire—you are achieving something you want, even if it is not what you want consciously. Recall the quote from the Upanishads:*
>
> *"You are what your deep, driving desire is. As your desire is, so is your will. As your will is, so is your deed. As your deed is, so is your destiny."*
>
> *In other words, what you have (and don't have, in short, your destiny) is the result of what you really, really want!*

For complete instructions read The Vikalpa Exercise beginning on page 146 in *The Four Desires*.

Step 1. In the space that follows, **write the one category of desire your intuition identified** at the end of The Bliss Meditation that you wrote in the oval on page 34.

_____

Step 2. Contemplate that your life is over. You are no longer alive; there is nothing more that you can do with the life that was yours.

> *Take those words in slowly. Consider the full weight of them. There is no more living to be done, no good-byes, no luggage or precious things that you can take with you. What is done is done. What is not done, is not. What is left are the facts of what you did and what you did not do. What is left is the evidence of what you really, really wanted—your Deepest Driving Desire.*

Now, you will bear witness as someone who cares and knows everything about you, eulogizes you and your life (you will provide their voice, just as you did in your testimonials). In the afterlife you will be able to hear everything they say, you will learn new things, be reminded of things you knew; you will come face to face with the person you were, not the person you wished to become—as you were in the Testimonial Exercise.

Choose the person you wish to eulogize you. It can be, but does not necessarily have to be, the same person who delivered your testimonial in that specific category of desire in The Dharma Code Exercise. They will eulogize you based only on the particular desire you identified in step 1, from your *sankalpa* Mind Map. You will only write one eulogy, not four, on just the one category of desire in the center of your Mind Map.

Step 3. **Write your eulogy.** It should be just a page or two. On page 39 & 40 of this workbook there is space for you to write. Imagine the speaker addressing the gathering of friends and family. His/her eulogy is straightforward; this person knows everything about you. Don't hold anything back when you write. The next few pages offer you some tips and questions to help you get started.

Your eulogy should:

- ❖ Be full of wisdom, compassion and caring

- ❖ Include accomplishments AND lack of accomplishments, specifically in that category of desire

- ❖ Consist of a real and completely honest review of how you lived, <u>not</u> how you would've liked to have lived

- ❖ Emphasize the differences from your testimonial written to uncover your DC

Include all of these in your eulogy:

- ❖ Words and thoughts about yourself and your life

- ❖ Beliefs and feelings that you may have kept to yourself

- ❖ Things you've finished

- ❖ Things started but not completed

- ❖ Things hoped for, but never started/acted upon

Tips for writing:

- ❖ Be straightforward

- ❖ Paint a clear picture of you in the context of your *sankalpa's category of* desire

- ❖ Take into account the speaker's insights about you, your thoughts about yourself and life, the beliefs and feelings you may have never shared with anyone else.

- ❖ Remember, the person eulogizing you knows everything about you:

    - ○ What you did
    - ○ What you didn't do
    - ○ Your aspirations
    - ○ Disappointments
    - ○ Hopes

If it's helpful, consider the following questions before you begin writing your eulogy.

- ❖ What one or two outstanding memories does the speaker have of you related to this particular desire?

- ❖ To what extent did your actions reflect your wants? What did you want to do, yet never manage to do? What hopes, aspirations, and intentions were never fulfilled? Why?

- ❖ What were the effects of your actions, including the ones you didn't take? Whom did they hurt?

- ❖ What price did you pay for not taking the actions that would have led toward you fulfilling your desires in this category?

- ❖ How often and why did you (or did you not) fulfill the particular desire through the course of your life?

- ❖ What does the speaker consider your greatest accomplishments and your greatest failures?

- ❖ Who was most helped or most hurt by your actions and in what ways?

- ❖ **MOST IMPORTANTLY:** If you failed to fully pursue your dream(s) related to this particular category of desire, what did you achieve by not pursuing it?

Time 15-20 min

My Eulogy Write as fast and as much as you can, leaving nothing out. Keep writing. Don't think or judge.

Once finished writing your eulogy, you may want to take a short break to relax and absorb what the exercise has revealed thus far. Go outside, have some comfort food, take some deep breaths or take a short walk, meditate or do something else to clear your head. Then come back and complete the exercise.

Step 4. Have your eulogy in front of you, along with a pen or highlighter. As you read through it, highlight or circle the words and phrases that seem the most significant in describing your life until now. Which of your goals in this category of desire have you accomplished and which you have not?

Please go to page 150 in *The Four Desires* to read an example of the words and phrases that Evan highlighted.

> *Consider this: in the instances where you did not fulfill your conscious desires, examine the evidence for what desires you <u>did</u> fulfill by not achieving or actively pursuing your conscious desires.*
>
> *A couple of examples: perhaps the eulogy reveals that you avoided taking the risks necessary to achieve the things you "wanted;" you may not have gotten what you consciously desired, but you may have fulfilled your desire to feel "safe." Your desire for security was fulfilled, even as your conscious desire of wanting a bigger, more expansive, expressive and creative life was not. Another example might be that your eulogy showed that you consistently didn't respond to your conscience, which negatively impacted your health or growth. Another version might be that you fulfilled the desire to keep the people around you comfortable, or avoid challenging your family's low expectations of you.*
>
> *I hope this is clear, because this is where this exercise is leading. Priceless discovery awaits you when you uncover the desire that has been actively shaping your destiny until now. Remember: "You are what your deep, driving desire is. As your desire is, so is your will. As your will is, so is your deed. As your deed is, so is your **destiny.**"*

This is how you find the clues to your *vikalpa—the desire or the "rule"* that you have been following above all others. If you apply the steps outlined below you will be led to discover them. The highlighted words and phrases from your eulogy will help you identify the Deepest Driving Desire that has shaped your life until now.

Next, read Sarah's story on page 138-141 in *The Four Desires* as another example of how a *vikalpa* can move you in the opposite direction of your conscious intentions.

Step 5. In the space that follows, write down all the words and phrases you highlighted in your eulogy. These will be used to identify your Deepest Driving Desire—the *vikalpa* that has been shaping your choices.

In the grid below, please write down all the words and phrases that you highlighted in your eulogy.

"Awareness is the beginning of change. " – Rod Stryker

Identify your *Vikalpa*

The word *vikalpa* means "thought construct." It refers to the kind of thoughts that disconnect you from what is true: from your heart, from abiding in Truth and your true place in the universe. It is what keeps you from being at home with yourself and your life. This exercise culminates in identifying your *vikalpa* that is hidden in your eulogy. Your intention is to recognize the source desire at the root of your non-constructive patterns. Thus, it is critical that your *vikalpa*'s final form needs to be stated as an "I want…" statement. It's tempting to avoid this approach, and perhaps harder to determine how you could "want" to not have the very thing you say you want, but that is why it is crucial that you create a *vikalpa* as a desire—<u>not</u> a label!

> *For instance, a vikalpa is not: "I am the child of an alcoholic," or "I have low self-esteem". These are just labels that are commonly used to explain why we do or do not act in our own best interests, why we do or don't have the things we want. The fact is that while that may be true, these kinds of labels do not determine behavior—after all, sometimes children of alcoholics go on to become incredibly successful and sometimes they don't. Labels do not determine behavior; desire determines behavior. Desire (or vasana) is the source of every action and every thought. Only after you isolate the desire that is keeping you from doing what you want to do, or not doing what you don't want to do, can you act on your consciously chosen positive desires that will lead you toward fulfilling your dharma. Thus, you must first identify the Deepest Driving Desire or vikalpa and recognize the power it has over you.*

After reading Sarah and Evan's stories, you can clearly see that they both wanted something, but their unconscious desires were not supporting their conscious intention*s* or their *dharmas*. As we have said, it's critical to remember that living from a *vikalpa*, despite its negative or harmful effects, provides some pay off. Therefore, it's critical to acknowledge the desire that is the heart of your *vikalpa,* if you are going to get past it and have what you really, really want.

Your job now is to recognize your Deepest Driving Desire and what its payoff has been up to this point. Before you try to write your *vikalpa*, use the next page to discover what you DID achieve—it may not be what you believe you wanted, nonetheless write what you did get… It should be in your eulogy. In Evan's case, he suffered tremendous health related consequences, but he managed to exact some pain (even, revenge) on his father. In Sarah's case, she was alone, but she managed to avoid being hurt by someone whom she loved.

Now, it's your turn…

> *This practice of self-analysis is precious, sacred, and profound work, often revealing the long hidden source of ancient patterns. Not surprisingly, there is innate resistance to uncovering and admitting to them, even if it is only to ourselves. But, that is precisely why this work has the potential to unlock new worlds and to close the door on being a prisoner of the past. Be courageous, venture forward and gain the insight necessary to step into a new freedom, new elegance and capacity. You stand at a turning point, where you can gain true mastery over your life and destiny.*

In the space below list the negative outcome(s) that your eulogy revealed (sick, alone, broke, unfulfilled, angry, fearful, creatively stuck, addicted, aimless, disempowered, spiritually empty—these are just some examples). Despite it being less than positive, I did achieve or become:

_____

_____

_____

_____

_____

_____

Please note: No one wants to suffer as an end in itself. Evan did not want to suffer physically for the sake of suffering, Sarah did not want to be alone, just to be alone. In both cases they got something from being sick or not being with someone. So, don't stop when you are at something like: "I wanted to be sick." "I wanted to avoid being successful." It's true that Evan was willing to pay a huge toll on his health, but what he really did want was to avenge his father's wrongs; Sarah didn't want to be alone, but she really, really did want to avoid being hurt by someone she loved.

Now it is time to acknowledge the underlying desire that has negatively determined your actions and decisions. In other words, you are going to identify the single sabotaging <u>desire</u>—that is at the root of the non-constructive patterns, feelings and beliefs found in your eulogy. Yes, it is time to recognize your vikalpa—the very thing that led you to your less than ideal circumstances.

Your *vikalpa is a statement that must begin with the words "I want..." (this is non* -negotiable). This approach has evolved since the book's release. Working with the vikalpas of countless students, I found that phrasing a vikalpa as an "I want" statement is critical to gain the insights necessary to overcome your obstacles and move you closer to your goals. Therefore, please do not refer to the <u>examples of</u> **<u>vikalpas</u> in *The Four Desires* book**. Lacking *"I want...,"* they are a list of labels, which will not move the needle toward positive change.

---

1. *WHAT DID YOU REALLY WANT? It's time to identify the desire that led you to the negative outcome that was your answer on the previous page. To do this, reflect on the following question:* **What did I get out of having achieved or become that outcome?** *This question can be phrased in different ways such as:* **What did I get out of it? What did it give me? What did it provide? How did this serve me?**
    Ask the questions as many times as necessary, until you have your answer to what it is you really wanted. Then, write what you got out of it below:

    _____

    _____

    _____

2. *Once again, write the less than desirable outcome that you achieved or became. What negative outcome did your eulogy reveal to you? This is your answer from the previous page.*

    _____

    _____

    _____

Once you have your answer to the above questions, you have your *vikalpa*:

I want (answer 1 above) _____

so, (answer 2 above)_____

See Appendix B at the back of this workbook to read some examples of *vikalpa*s. Like in the **examples of the DC's, they are there for your reference, it's important to note that <u>none of these examples is your *vikalpa*</u>**. Yours is unique to you. Please review them to get a sense of the range and form that they can take and what an effective *vikalpa* can look like. You'll absolutely still need to create your own.

Now, write your *vikalpa*, one more time, exactly so that the form of it is consistent with the examples in the Appendix B. First, the pay off (or what you actually wanted), then the price you were willing to pay.

_____

_____

_____

_____

_____

> *Congratulations! At this point you should have your vikalpa. Now take a short break. That was a huge accomplishment!*

Please note: There's a good chance you have more than one *vikalpa*. For now and especially if this is your first experience with this exercise, please focus on unearthing just one. Later in the workbook you may uncover more resistance and as you repeat *The Four Desires* process you will identify other *vikalpas*.

The fact is that most students are not able to fully develop their authentic and effective DC until they view it through the lens of their *vikalpa*! Before going any further, you will need to review your DC in light of your *vikalpa*. So, with your *vikalpa* in full view, it's time to review your DC.

! Read page 154 in *The Four Desires*, Your Dharma Code is the Cure to Your *Vikalpa*.

These will be the last steps to ensure that your DC truly embraces the totality of you, so that it affirms your unique capacities and empowers you to overcome your challenges. Use the following strategies to clarify, strengthen and expand the reach of your DC and, in so doing, resolve your *vikalpa*:

1. Look back and compare your *vikalpa* to your DC.

> *Your DC must have something in it that addresses and is the cure for your vikalpa. In other words, if you were to completely honor your DC would it resolve the stuff of your vikalpa? Both should be very clear calls to action—one helpful and one not helpful. If your DC does not specifically resolve your vikalpa—and, most first DC drafts <u>do not</u> resolve the vikalpa—you have some work to do to ensure that it does.*

2. You are going to circle or write down all the negative words (key concepts or phrases) from your *vikalpa*. Your intention is to isolate these negative terms, words, ideas and verbs. Once this is done, once you've isolated the negative/destructive ideas and concepts, you will ensure that your DC has the positive and constructive elements within it to resolve them. You will look closely at how to evolve your DC, and what it specifically needs so you can be (and act) free of these negative patterns. The next page will walk you through this critical part of the process.

3. Make sure your DC is written with enough power, enthusiasm and yes, even passion to negate your *vikalpa*. After doing battle with these less than ideal desires, for who knows how long, you'll want to arm yourself with the right words and intentions so you can win the inner conflict of fully honoring your soul's purpose. Reword and rework your DC until it cures and is more powerful than your *vikalpa*.

4. Remember that your DC is more than a cure for what ails you, it should also include all those luscious dreams and aspirations you acknowledged in the previous works, highlighted by your poem, three words, and themes found in your testimonials. So, this is also a good time to review your DC and confirm that it includes these vital aspirational nuggets, if not, your DC will need an additional piece(s).

> *As you continue to apply the work of The Four Desires, new insights into your patterns and subsequent vikalpas will be revealed to you. Thus, you will need to consider whether or not your DC, in its current state, resolves your additional vikalpas. By continuing to stay open and self-aware you will eventually arrive at your final and true DC.*

Before you begin the work of comparing your DC and vikalpa, let's go through the steps one by one and examine a real life example of a student's at one of my Four Desires Workshops.

1. The first step is to write down the vikalpa; this was hers:

> *"I want to diminish my own light, so I don't have to answer the call of my Heart; I want to prove my mom right, that I am unworthy and will never amount to anything."*

2. The next step is to circle or highlight the most negative, insidious and destructive ideas within it; here are her highlighted words:

> *"I want to **diminish my own light**, so I **don't** have to **answer the call of my heart**; I want to **prove my mom** right, that **I am unworthy** and will **never amount to anything.***

3. You will then write each of these words or phrases separately. These are the key negative terms/concepts in her vikalpa, that she is seeking to resolve:

- *diminish my own light,*
- *(don't) ...answer the call of my heart*
- *prove my mom*
- *I am unworthy*
- *never amount to anything*

4. Next, you will review each negative or counter-productive concept and ensure that there is language in your DC that addresses/resolves each one. Let's take a close look at our example; this is her DC:

> *"Answering the call of my Heart, I fearlessly share the full magnitude of my Being with the world. I trust in God and myself above all others. I believe in me, therefore I have everything I need to be supremely, joyfully me."*

The following is exactly the process I used to help her finalize her DC in light of her vikalpa(s).

❖ Read the first sentence of her DC, "Answering the call of my Heart, I fearlessly share the full magnitude of my Being with the world." Clearly this statement resolves the first two negative ideas "(diminish my own light") and "(don't... answer the call of my heart") as well as the last one ("never amount to anything").

❖ Her next sentence: "I trust in God and myself above all others" resolves, "prove to mom" and "I am unworthy." In fact, it sounds as though throughout her DC, she's "amounted" to something of real value.

❖ Finally, and for good measure, there's her final statement, "I believe in me, therefore I have everything I need to be supremely, joyfully me."

> *I believe she uncovered a powerful and vibrant DC; one that really works. She has satisfied all the critical requirements of a DC. Her DC cures all the points in her vikalpa. Her DC addresses all four categories of desires and, for good measure; she's even managed to get "joy" into it. Awesome! I am certain the prospect of committing to her new DC excited her as soon as she crafted it, and that she could immediately sense the power and value of making her DC her new Deepest Driving Desire. To the extent that she does, it will change everything.*
>
> **Until you apply this approach and make the necessary adjustments to your DC, you will not (and can not) have a completely authentic and fully useful DC. It's that simple.**

* For a list of DC examples, that were similarly refined in light of curing *vikalpa*, see Appendix C.

Now it's your turn. Here, you will apply the exact same process. Be painstaking and thorough. Once you have completed the process, you will have set the stage for extraordinary and positive changes.

1. The first step is to write down your *vikalpa*:

_____

_____

_____

_____

2. The next step is to circle or highlight the most negative, insidious and destructive ideas within it.

3. In the space below please write down each idea you just highlighted (you may have more, you may have less, than six):

- _____

- _____

- _____

- _____

- _____

- _____

4. Now it's time to review and match up the phrases, words, or statements in your DC that address/resolve each destructive idea above. There are many ways to complete this step. One option is to rewrite your DC in the space below, then circle or highlight the specific parts of it that are the antidotes to each *vikalpa* bullet point above and draw a line to that bullet point and cross it out.

_____

_____

_____

_____

_____

_____

5. After completing this step, if you find that any of the *vikalpa* bullet points are not covered in your DC, then your DC needs more refinement and/or additional pieces. The good news: what it needs is right in front of you and already within you.

! On the next page you will find space to do your DC final refinements.

Use this page to write and rewrite your DC as a cure for your *vikalpa*. You will also add whatever additional pieces it needs, so that your DC accomplishes all that it is meant to accomplish (however, you don't want your DC to be so long that you cannot easily recall it).

Write your DC below.

_____

_____

_____

_____

Now read it out loud to yourself or someone you trust; listen to the words carefully. Is it as clear as it could be? Is there better, more precise language to convey the core of its meaning, the vision that you want it to portray? Ultimately, it needs to be able to lead you to the end result detailed in your testimonials. The space below is your opportunity to make it even better.

_____

_____

_____

_____

Now read over your DC again.

Ask yourself, "are the critical points in the right order?" It's amazing how much the sequence of the words within a single sentence or in the sentences themselves (if you have more than one) can take it from being close, to exactly what it needs to be. Be precise—your DC is your marching orders for you to live your best life. Striving for clarity and excellence is key for you arriving at your true DC. So, now look at it with the intention of finding the best order for all your DC's content and write the best version of it below.

_____

_____

_____

_____

Below is a checklist of things that your DC must meet in order to be the most effective. Put a check mark next to each one if your DC meets it.

Dharma Code:

_____

_____

_____

_____

I. Your Dharma Code must:

☐ **ADDRESS YOUR SOUL'S JIVA** (UNIQUE JOURNEY). Thus, your DC can include <u>only</u> one of the following three words: Love, give, serve.

☐ **BE EXPANSIVE ENOUGH TO TOUCH ALL OF YOUR LIFE.** Be certain it addresses and will impact all four categories of desires, unlike your *sankalpa*, which should address primarily only one of the four desires.

☐ **BE PRACTICAL.** If someone were to read it, would they understand it? If not, consider if you need to clarify your DC. Put the essential elements of the description that you said out loud into your DC. There's no question about Gandhi's DC. "I shall not fear anyone on Earth, I shall fear only God. I shall not bear ill toward anyone. I shall not submit to injustice from anyone. I shall conquer untruth by truth, and in resisting untruth, I shall put up with all suffering." This is not to say that you are writing your DC for other people's consumption. But even so, it must be so clear that it delineates a crystalline and purposeful path of action. If it's too flowery, it's not practical.

☐ **BE ACTIONABLE.** It is, by definition, a statement, which if you were to embody it, if it were to truly guide your actions, speech and thoughts, it would propel you to fully express the totality of your soul's wisdom and power.

☐ **TOUCH YOUR CORE.** Does your DC elicit a strong visceral response? Does the prospect of committing to it create excitement or fear or perhaps both? It's a good sign if it does.

☐ **MOVE YOU FROM THEORY TO REALITY.** Would committing to your DC resolve your vikalpa? This is critical and absolutely required! It must move you past your patterns and help you to truly learn your life lessons and thrive. Furthermore, if you were to serve your DC completely, would it propel you through your challenges? Please note: if later you find more *vikalpas* arise, you may need to add another phrase or sentence to your DC to ensure it is complete.

☐ **BE BIGGER THAN YOUR OBSTACLES.** If you were to spend the next few decades serving your DC, would it lead you to accomplish all that you described in your four testimonials?

☐ **NURTURE YOU AND THE WHOLE OF CREATION.** Will your DC guide you to serve your highest best interests and, in the process, empower you to serve the universal *dharma*?

Now that you've identified your VK and DC, you are ready to create your *sankalpa*, the goal you will accomplish in the next 6-18 months. Turn the page to finish the steps of The Sankalpa Exercise.

Step 5. Create a mind map containing your spontaneous positive associations to fulfilling the specific category of desire that your soul has selected.

Read pages 102-104 in *The Four Desires* for a full explanation of Step 5. Once you have, then continue with the exercise below.

Your *sankalpa*, unlike your DC, is a specific intention, one that generally targets only one category of desire. For your sankalpa, I suggest focusing on a specific intention that you plan on achieving in the next 6-18 months. It should be a goal that is definitely attainable, yet worthy and significant enough that it will require you to put forward your best efforts to bring it to fruition.

Recall the category of desire you wrote in the oval on page 34. You're going to complete that mind map now, First, write that desire in the oval below. Consider how fulfillment in that category touches you and your life. How will it affect you for the better?

Then, draw a single line extending from the oval. On it, write the first word that comes to mind associated to the fulfillment of that desire. Continue to draw one line at a time and fill them in with word(s) until you have 10-12 words radiating from your desire. Be fast, not careless. (You can read Step 6 on page 104 & to see Eric's example in the *The Four Desires*).

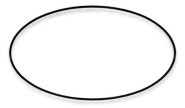

You will now survey all the associated words to the category of desire that you jotted down. Take 1 minute to inventory your mind map, allow your intuition to consider the full picture—some words on your mind map may be very familiar, but there may also be aspects about the fulfillment of that category of desire you may not have ever considered.

The Four Desires Workbook

It's time for you to determine, your specific goal/*sankalpa*. You may already know what it is. Your goal may jump out at you immediately or, in many cases, it will take a little more consideration to identify the precise goal that your intuition is pointing you toward achieving. Reviewing your mind map, you'll allow the words, in the context of the category of desire, to gestate. Again, remember that the context of your *sankalpa* is based on the question: "What one desire, if it were fulfilled in the next 6-18 months, would best serve my *dharma*?"

Step 6. Specify the particular goal your soul is prompting you to achieve. Again, look at the Mind Map you just created, it is time to determine the particular goal or intention your soul is prompting you to achieve. Hint: It may help if you consider what you will need to accomplish in real terms in order to achieve the sense of what these words are describing. In other words, what measurable accomplishment/change would provide you with the qualities outlined by the words in your mind map? At this point just identify that goal—don't concern yourself with the best way to write it yet.

What do those words tell you that you long to become or achieve? To what specific goal are the words pointing?

_____

_____

_____

_____

_____

Once your specific goal is clear, you will write a short description of a scene that depicts you having accomplished that desire. As you envision fulfilling this desire, be specific, feel it, see it. Let it become so real that you can experience the unique feelings (and perhaps even emotions) that bubble up. Include your feelings/emotions as well as the material details in your description of what it is like to fulfill your desire. Having an emotional association plays a vital role in empowering your *sankalpa*.

On the following page, write 2-3 paragraphs describing in detail your experience of having achieved your *sankalpa*.

Time: 10 minutes

Now, make the vision of fulfilling your desire even more tangible. On this page, you have the option of creating a graphic vision of your desires fulfilled. If you aren't inspired to draw, create a collage by attaching magazine pictures, photos and other images that represent the fulfillment of your *sankalpa*. You have the option of drawing the scene you just wrote about. You don't need to be an artist, just sketch any images associated to it, even stick figures will do. Allow this scene to flow through you. Have fun. Use colored pencils to make it even more vivid. Take a few minutes to create the scene; it doesn't need to take you a long time.

Achieve Something Great: 1st Draft of Your Sankalpa *adapted from TFD pg. 106*

Finding the best way to word your *sankalpa* can be difficult. However, by following each of the steps described below, finding the specific intention and the right words to describe it will be incredibly easy.

> *Once you've created a clear sense of what it will look and feel like to achieve your desire, the words for your sankalpa will present themselves to you—effortlessly—trust me. Just follow these steps, without getting ahead of me.*

Read over the description; look at the images you've drawn. You should now have the answers to these two questions:

• **What do I specifically want to achieve or become?**

• **What will having what I want look and feel like?**

Step 7. Draft your *sankalpa*. The easiest and most powerful way to create your *sankalpa* is to feel the full force of having achieved it, sense the joy, the victory of it, sense how your life is affected by having fulfilled your *sankalpa*.

Now imagine you get a phone call from a good friend you haven't talked to in a while. Early in the conversation your friend says, "You sound great! Different. Tell me, what's happened since we talked last?"
In the moment, the news just pours out of you. You tell them exactly what has happened.
Tell him or her in one, possibly two sentences what has occurred. Don't hesitate to include the feelings you are experiencing as it relates to it.

To complete the exercise, own all of your feelings and thoughts about achieving your goal. Now the phone rings and you tell your friend what has happened, why you sound so different.

Here's an example, in the book Eric's *sankalpa*: "Free at last! The business sold before the first of the year. It worked out perfectly for us and the buyer. We are all thriving." *For more examples see Appendix D.

Please, write, in the space below, your *SANKALPA*, exactly how you would describe to a friend having achieved something important to you.

_____

_____

_____

_____

Once you are done, you should have a statement that:

- ❖ Details the specific results you want to achieve and, quite possibly, the attitudes that will accompany it.

- ❖ Actively states, in present (or past) tense, something that sounds like a fact that has already occurred.

- ❖ Sounds like something you would actually say.

! Now that you have a *sankalpa*, look at the guidelines in Appendix D at the back of the workbook on page 98 & 99. Does it meet them? If not, reword it. Remember, a DC describes a general approach to life. A *sankalpa* is specific, a tangible goal achievable in the next 6-18 months.

Once you fulfill this sankalpa, I strongly recommend creating a new sankalpa, for your next intention, so you can continue fulfilling your Dharma.

Since The Four Desires was published, I've taught a second option for crafting the language of sankalpa. I call it the "old-age" approach, as opposed to the style on the previous page, which I refer to as the "new age approach." You can use either, it's up to you—whichever of the two feels like it will be a stronger, more potent call to action. In the "new-age approach" you just walked through, you crafted language that was present or past tense, with the objective of sending your unconscious a clear message. You avoided using future tense, like "I want to stop smoking." Since we never arrive at the future, this can appear to be passive and less effective. However, the fact is most of us get things done, especially objectives that are challenging, by telling ourselves something like, "I can stop smoking, I will stop smoking, I must stop smoking." In other words, we empower ourselves ("I can"), we assure ourselves of our intention ("I will"), and commit ourselves to the concept that failure is not an option ("I must").

In this, the old-age approach, you will draw from these three phrases (I can..., I will..., I must...,) to create three distinct sentences. Like in the following example:

I can sell the business before the first of the year.
I will sell the business before the first of the year.
I must sell the business before the first of the year

Try it. Simply take the sankalpa you wrote on the previous page and in the space below write it out as three separate sentences with, "I can, I will, I must" as the first words of each statement.

_____
_____
_____
_____
_____
_____

"Declaring what you want is only the first step..." – Rod Stryker

Please read chapter 11 in *The Four Desires*. In these pages is an unfailing formula that explains the principle of attainment, how we move (or don't move) from desire to fulfillment. I call it The Creation Equation. This formula identifies three key elements involved in attaining your wants, goals & dreams:

Below are some questions to help you reflect and understand The Creation Equation.

1. Below, write down the formula that is The Creation Equation.

2.In your own words, explain what this formula means.

3. Describe the concept of each Sanskrit word used in The Creation Equation.

❖ *Shakti*

❖ *Vayu*

❖ *Karma*

❖ *Prapti*

> *In the pages after Chapter II in The Four Desires, our focus moves from creating a blueprint for fulfillment to its realization. Applying the principles of The Creation Equation will ensure that you embody and continuously live according to your DC and achieve your sankalpa. Be patient, keep up the good work and complete all of the exercises to come, particularly if you have felt challenged or resistant to any of the previous practices and exercises.*

Master Your Destiny: Meditation to Increase Shakti

"Your soul is pure, boundless creative energy or Shakti." – Rod Stryker

The Meditation to Increase *Shakti* will help you easily and effectively access your soul's power or *shakti*. You can read instructions on page 134 in *The Four Desires*, and the companion CD contains an introduction as well as guided practice. Please practice it as often as you'd like to build your connection to greater inner strength, wisdom and creative energy. Fill in the log here whenever you do this meditation.

Date	Duration	Reflection

The Four Desires Workbook

Read the story on pages 152 & 153 in *The Four Desires* about the man "holding on" (to a tree). This story reminds us of just how easy it is to *not* "let go," even if doing so is unproductive or perhaps, even self-destructive. The message is clear. You will need to apply self-effort to change your patterns and extract yourself from the things to which you are negatively attached. After you are finished reading the story, reflect on a time in your life when you were proactive—where you exerted your will and managed to change a negative or destructive pattern and thereby, changed your destiny.

In the space below write three paragraphs about it:

     1.   In the first paragraph describe your "tree," what you needed to change or let go of and why.

     2.   In the second paragraph write about what you did to extricate yourself from or change the pattern.

     3.   In the last paragraph (it can be more than one, if you want) write about the outcome of your positive efforts (materially, emotionally and spiritually). Describe the different future you created by actively changing your present.

If you prefer you can write a poem about it, otherwise write a minimum of 3 paragraphs.

"Awareness is the beginning of change." – Rod Stryker

Take five minutes to make a simple list. Later you will use it as part of a powerful and pivotal exercise, so please be as thorough as possible.

Time: 5 min
Make a list of all the ways you expend your time or energy non-constructively.

Although, in the book this exercise is called Listing Your Bad Habits, I prefer not calling this a list of bad habits, because not all the ways you waste time and energy are necessarily "bad" in and of themselves. You can include bad habits but, your list should include more than your biggest, most obvious bad habits; it should also include any and all ways that you waste your time and energy.

❖ See if you can come up with at least 10-15 things, more if you are able

❖ Include any and all bad habits that you recognize as being less than constructive

❖ Write everything that you do regularly that you would be better off not doing

❖ The use of technology such as talking on the phone, texting or checking email, not to mention, television—all of which can become a waste of time and an unproductive use of energy

❖ Here are some common examples to remember to include if you do them: too much talk radio, social media, television, over-working, gossiping, snacking on foods that deplete your energy, not exercising, exercising too much, drinking multiple cups of coffee every day, pornography, gossip magazines, not going to sleep early enough...

Below and on the next page is space for you to list your habits:

Master Your Destiny: List Your Habits

Master Your Destiny: Relax Into Greatness

"When you become established in complete effortlessness and ease,
where past and future burdens are dissolved, your unconscious becomes more open
and available to respond to your conscious desires." – Rod Stryker

Relax Into Greatness is a practice of systematic deep relaxation. It heals the body, rejuvenates the mind and awakens the mind's higher potentials, including intuition. You can read more about Relax Into Greatness starting on page 160 in *The Four Desires*. You will learn how it is the perfect practice to combine with *sankalpa* and thereby, seed your resolution deep into your subconscious. Practice it at least 2-3 times a week. Use this space to keep a log of your experience while you are completing *The Four Desires*.

> *I recommend doing Relax Into Greatness, by listening to it on the companion CD.*

Date	Duration	Reflection

The Four Desires Workbook

This exercise will help you identify any additional resistance or negative patterns. Read pages 172-173 in *The Four Desires* for instructions on how to identify additional *vikalpas*.

5 min
For the next 5 minutes write your *sankalpa* over and over and over again.

- ❖ Use the exact same words each time, notice how you feel as you write the words. As long as you can believe or feel positive about what you're writing, continue to do so.

- ❖ The moment you hear or sense any objection, disbelief or resistance to your *sankalpa*, write down that opposing thought or feeling. Be brief. Don't analyze your objections; just write down whatever comes up. Write all of the dialogue that your subconscious rattles off.

- ❖ Then for the remainder of the time, keep writing your *sankalpa* unless you hear or feel more objections to it.

Try This:
Practice The Hidden Resistance Exercise at least once a week and watch how resistance changes over time.

"If you don't consciously choose the direction of your life,
your past will choose it for you." – Rod Stryker

You'll now turn to the practices of Departure Point and Seeding the Gap. Both of these techniques will help you continue building momentum toward acting on your DC and fulfilling your *sankalpa*. You've done the essential work necessary for self-discovery, now applying the next two steps are vital to solidify your previous efforts, to turn away from the old you and thus, welcome your new, purposeful and better future. Read more about these techniques on pages 179-180 in *The Four Desires*. Use the steps listed below as reference.

Step 1: Create Your Departure Point

❖ Choose a habit to give up from the list you created on page 68 & 69 of this workbook.

❖ Choose one that's deeply ingrained and has a strong enough hold on you that giving it up will be meaningful. In other words, by giving it up you will be creating some new space in your life. The habit you choose needs to be something you do regularly—preferably something you do or think about daily.

❖ Know with certainty that you can give it up, are willing to give it up. If giving it up seems too overwhelming, and you have serious doubts that you will be able to, choose a different habit.

❖ It is preferable to give up a habit that you <u>do</u>, rather than a habit that you <u>think</u>—actions are easier to track than thoughts, thus it will be easier to measure whether or not you've actually stopped doing it.

❖ Your departure point does not have to be, but can be directly related to your *sankalpa* (for example, if your *sankalpa* has to do with losing weight, you don't have to choose one that relates to your diet—you can, but it is not required).

❖ You don't have to give up your habit entirely for this exercise to be effective. For example, if you waste time checking email, however you need to check it for business, then commit to a reasonable amount say, 3 times per day, instead of the 35 times a day that you have been checking your email.

❖ Don't beat yourself up if you fall back under the sway of your habit. The aim of this exercise, to disrupt your old momentum and patterns, can be quite difficult. It requires sustained self-effort to follow through and implement lasting change. Anyone can do it for a few days or weeks. But, until you sustain the new behavior for at least 40 days, it won't be engrained enough to get you past the old behavior.

❖ Even a habit that is less than consequential and is relatively easy enough to give up can be challenging. By letting go of even an inconsequential habit, you are changing your trajectory and giving yourself the opportunity to "seed" your unconscious with the positive desire or intention of your *sankalpa* (or DC). Just remember that when you do make even a small dent in your unconscious behaviors, it is a wonderful gift to yourself that will have the effect of moving you in the direction of achieving your true desires.

> **IMPORTANT POINT:** *Since the book's release, I have changed my recommendation for how you apply Departure Point and Seeding the Gap. I strongly advise you to use your DC, instead of your sankalpa, for the first 40 days of implementing these two practices. Since your DC touches on the totality of your life, it is critical that you first establish it as your foundation, and only then move onto your short term goals—your sankalpa. For a minimum of 40 days, plant your DC into the gap created by not engaging in your habit. Once your deeper and more all-encompassing patterns have shifted, practice seeding your sankalpa in the gap.*

Step 2: Seed the Gap

❖ At some point, perhaps many times during the day, you will have an impulse to engage your habit.

❖ Rather than satisfy the impulse, stop.

❖ At this instant, turn your attention away from your impulse to engage in the habit and toward a Higher Source, a source of peace and calm, infinite intelligence, God, nature, or even a remembrance of the love and support of people to whom you are closest.

❖ For an instant, rest in this experience. Relax. Surrender to it. Be nowhere other than right there.

❖ Now, mindful of that experience of your Higher Source, recall your DC or your *sankalpa*. Mentally repeat the precise words, while you remember the feelings as well as the image you associate with it. With full feeling and knowledge, have the certainty and confidence that you embody the powerful truths of your DC or that your *sankalpa* has already been fulfilled.

❖ Give thanks and cultivate a powerful sense of gratitude.

"Your future is your past modified by your present. " – Rod Stryker

Once you've completed:

      1.) Uncovering your Mighty Purpose & created your DC,
      2.) Unearthing your *vikalpa*
      3.) Creating a *sankalpa*

It is time to ensure that the work will carry over into your life and that your future is going to be truly different than your past. Consider this as a model for approaching your destiny:

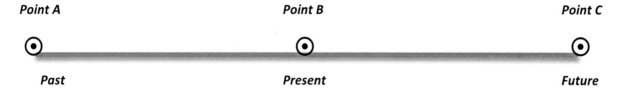

In order to create a new trajectory and get a different future, you must interrupt your current trajectory.

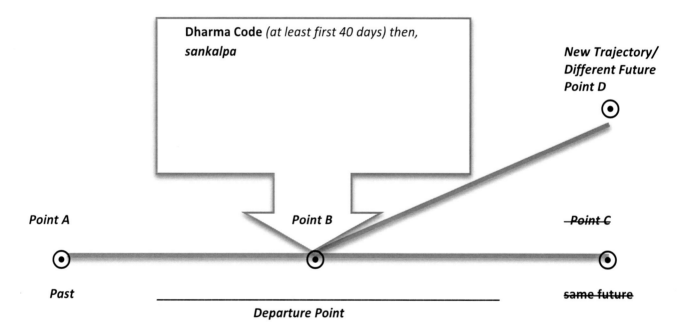

On the line directly above, write the habit you will use as your Departure Point. Inside the box above it, write your DC. Every time you find yourself about to indulge in the habit, take pause and Seed The Gap by mentally repeating your DC. Use this method for a minimum of 40 days.

Once the foundation of your DC is established, then use your *sankalpa* to Seed The Gap. As you continue to overcome your habits, come back to this space and pick a new habit as your departure point. When you accomplish your *sankalpa,* use the process again to create a new *sankalpa* and watch your future unfold as a life purposefully lived.

The Four Desires Workbook

"Stillness is a more compelling force to influence and attract, and thereby help you fulfill your desires, than is desperation or even willpower alone." – Rod Stryker

The Healing the Heart Meditation dissolves sadness, emotional pain and suffering; moreover it helps you reestablish your connection to eternal joy. You can read more about it on page 202 in *The Four Desires,* and the companion CD contains an introduction and guided practice by Rod. Please practice it as often as you'd like and keep a log here whenever you do this meditation.

Date	Duration	Reflection

The Four Desires Workbook

> *"For intuition to grow as a force in your life, you have to learn to honor it." – Rod Stryker*

Increasing your intuition is a two-part process:

❖ **Part one** is accessing your inner wisdom, that part of you that knows and is always at the ready to guide you to do precisely the right thing at precisely the right time; in Sanskrit it's called *dhi*. In order to access it, you must quiet mental activity on a regular basis, unload your worries and thoughts and finally, tap into a still and restful state of awareness.

❖ **Part two** is to consistently act on what your intuition is telling you.

> *Accessing intuitive knowledge takes practice, but gets easier the more you tap into it. The more you listen and act on what it tells you to do, the stronger your intuition will become.*

This practice of accessing your intuition follows the Healing the Heart Meditation from *The Four Desires* companion CD (or you can use any other meditation that helps to quiet your mind). Once you are aware of yourself resting in a sense of wholeness and contentment, you are ready to access your intuition. Use the following technique whenever you have a question or seek guidance about how to achieve your *sankalpa* or make any other important decision.

You tap into intuition, less by reaching for answers and more by trusting that the answers are already within you, just waiting to be recognized. Please read page 200-201 in *The Four Desires* for helpful tips on asking questions and advice about listening for answers.

It is imperative to first practice a meditation that quiets your thoughts such as the Healing the Heart Meditation. Then go through the steps below.

Step 1. Once your mind is quiet, just be there. Rest in a state of contentment and ease. Dissolve all doubt, insecurity and fear.

Step 2. Sense the presence of intuition. Feel this "knowing presence" become more concentrated and sense where it is located in your body. Take your awareness to this place and rest there.

Step 3. Abiding in this inner wisdom, assume you need to know nothing. Drop all expectation or the need for a particular answer. Be open to everything.

Step 4. Silently ask your question with clarity and precision. If you are unsure what to ask, try this, "What does my soul want me to know?"

Step 5. Remain completely relaxed and hold your awareness in your "wisdom center," then listen for an immediate response to your question. If you don't hear it or perceive it, center yourself and ask again. If after two attempts you still don't have an answer, return to Step 1.

Step 6. Once you have a clear definitive response, slowly come back. Acknowledge that you've been somewhere special and done something important. Thank your inner guide.

! Use the Daily Dhi Mind Map at the back of this workbook on page 100. To be able to hear, feel and allow your intuition to guide you, you need to access it weekly, if not on a daily basis.

"The single hardest yoga practice is the same for everyone. It's called change." – Rod Stryker

The directions for this exercise are very simple: Now or sometime in the near future when you are ready, dedicate forty-eight hours to say "yes" to the things your inner voice says "yes" to, and "no" to those things to which your inner voice says "no." In other words, listen to your inner guidance in all you do. ***Please wait to do this exercise until you are confident that you are able to hear, sense or see your inner voice and have had validation that what you are perceiving as your intuition is <u>always</u> correct and serving Dharma.*** Please read the last paragraph on page 219 to the beginning of the exercise on page 220 in *The Four Desires* for more information about when to do and when not to do this exercise.

Start where you are. If you're just starting to listen to *dhi* and feel forty-eight hours is too much then do this exercise for as long as you can. Once you can hear or sense your *dhi*, do a dedicated practice of fearless action. If you find that you don't want to stop, you can extend it for as long as you like. Very likely, you'll find it catapults you to an entirely new way of being: freer, more powerful, more often in the right place at the right time.

    ❖   **How many hours do you feel you can practice Fearless Action? _____**

Once the time comes to an end, use the space below to write about your experience. Reflect on following your *dhi*. Use the questions below to help you get a clearer idea about your relationship to "knowing what to do" and "doing what you know."

    ❖   In what ways were the last forty-eight hours different?

    ❖   How completely did you listen?

    ❖   How well did you respond to inner guidance?

❖ How often did you listen to it and how often did you not?

❖ Where were the particular areas of your life where you felt stuck or less responsive to your inner guidance?

❖ What did you learn from the exercise?

❖ What did it tell you about the way you live or the way you would like to live?

"Yoga is the breaking of contact with pain." – The Bhagavad Gita

At some point in life, we all ask ourselves questions like, "How do I remain positive and find joy while I wait for my dreams to be fulfilled?" "Where do I turn when things appear hopeless?" Throughout the ages, spiritual traditions have provided a single answer. In the west we call it surrender, letting go or non-attachment. The Sanskrit term for it is *vairagya*. To learn more about *vairagya* and freedom from fear read chapter 20 in *The Four Desires* beginning on page 229.

Time: 15 minutes
Step 1. Recall an experience in your past that had a significant negative impact on you. It can be any experience, circumstance, or condition that was emotionally, physically or spiritually hurtful or debilitating.

Step 2. On the next page, write one paragraph detailing what happened in that particular experience or event.

Step 3. Then below it, write another paragraph describing the aftermath of that particular experience or event. Detail the ways it has inhibited you or had a harmful or less than constructive impact on your life.

Tips for Writing:

❖ You can write about a childhood experience or something more contemporary.

❖ Write how the aftermath caused you to feel, think or act in ways that either sabotaged you or kept you from recognizing who you truly are and could be.

❖ It doesn't necessarily have to be your life's most dramatic or intense event, but can be.

❖ You don't have to choose an event that makes you feel emotionally overwhelmed or takes you to a dark emotional place.

❖ Only write two paragraphs: One, the details of what happened and two, the negative effects of that experience.

"The choices you make about how you will respond determine everything." – Rod Stryker

Read page 237-242 in *The Four Desires* to learn about perspective and Miracle Angle, then complete Part II of The Vairagya Exercise. On the next page, you will write about the same experience you wrote about in Part I of this exercise, but this time you will write one or two paragraphs about: How that experience has helped you, how it could help you or how it could contribute something to your life. In other words, you will look at it from a different perspective, your Miracle Angle.

Time: 15 minutes

Tips for Writing:

- ❖ Look at the experience now from the opposite or alternate perspective to the one you wrote in Part I.

- ❖ Begin writing only when you have found a perspective and a way of relating to the experience or event that is authentic. Take as long as you need to gain insight into how you can view it as contributing something constructive to your life.

- ❖ Write only about how it was or could be helpful, how it empowered or could empower you.

Here are some questions to ask yourself to help you decide what to write:

- ❖ What has the experience or event taught you?

- ❖ How has it strengthened you?

- ❖ How has it helped you in your relationships with other people?

- ❖ How has it helped you spiritually?

- ❖ Has it helped you become more compassionate, more ethical, more inspired, more capable?

- ❖ Has it helped you not take yourself or every setback in life too seriously?

When you're done writing the positive effects of the experience, ask yourself these questions:

❖ Were you able to find at least one positive way to view your circumstances?

❖ Was it hard to find?

❖ Until now, have you ever chosen to look at your experience from a positive perspective? If not, why not or, if so, how frequently?

❖ Have you consciously chosen not to or has it been an unconscious decision?

❖ Would it help you to start viewing it from this new perspective from this point forward?

❖ Is there anything to gain by not looking at it from this positive, healing, or proactive perspective?

> *"If you resist learning your lessons in their gentler forms,*
> *life is more than prepared to teach you through ever-increasing hardship." – Rod Stryker*

After the last exercise, you had a chance to experience first-hand what it's like to apply the first stage of non-attachment. On the other hand, if you found what you think is a Miracle Angle, but you feel that you are still not at peace with your situation, it means you are not living from it, yet.

Read Jennifer's Story on page 245 of *The Four Desires* as an example of how choosing to live from your Miracle Angle can make all the difference.

Stage two of non-attachment means staying open to learning about yourself, even as you wait for your dreams to come true and life's challenges to pass. Dreams don't happen because you dream them, they happen because you do something about them while remaining content in the journey and surrender to a higher purpose. In the process, you will become a fuller and more complete version of yourself.

The following are things you practice to create more *vairagya* and enjoy its benefits. Please use the next page in this workbook to reflect on your practice of these.

- ❖ **Practices to bring more benefits of *vairagya* to the external world, your relationships and circumstances:**

    - ○ Compromise, self-reflection, forgiveness, charity, humility, compassion, selfless service

- ❖ **Practices to bring more benefits of *vairagya* at the internal level:**

    - ○ Meditation, prayer, relaxation, Relax Into Greatness, calm breathing, asana practices, massage, self

        reflection

- ❖ **Practices to bring more benefits of *vairagya* to the spiritual level:**

    - ○ Prayer, devotion, meditation

*"Devotion and meditation are the best and most direct means to help you reach
the ultimate aim of vairagya, lasting peace." – Rod Stryker*

Throughout the process of *The Four Desires*, you learn that one of the keys to fulfillment is experiencing the part of you that can only be known by a still mind. Meditation is the essential methodology to lead you there. The Meditation Practice to Increase *Vairagya* is one of five different meditations offered in *The Four Desires*. You can read more about it on page 258. The companion CD contains an introduction and guided version. Practice as consistently as possible to increase your capacity to let go and to ultimately touch your soul. Use this space for reflection whenever you do this meditation.

Date	Duration	Reflection

"Reshape yourself through the power of your will." – from The Bhagavad Gita

Holding on to old habits, including thoughts, feelings and beliefs from a grievance angle, only serves to increase the amount of resistance in our lives. Once again, consider the Creation Equation: $I_s + I_v > I_k \approx P$

In order to achieve *Prapti*, to attain your goals, you must reduce the intensity of *karma* and increase the intensity of desire + the intensity of the process you apply to achieve that desire. Use the tables here to outline a plan for what you will do to increase *vairagya* then, use the form on pg. 101-102 of this workbook to hold yourself accountable to it.

Choose 1-3 techniques to focus on below to increase *vairagya* in your external world and environment:

Technique	Describe how you will apply 1-3 of the following techniques over the next 40 days.
Compromise	
Selfless Service	
Charity	
Humility	
Compassion	
Forgiveness	
Other	

Choose 1-3 techniques from the list below to increase *vairagya* internally:

Techniques	Describe how you will apply 1-3 of the following techniques over the next 40 days.
Meditation	
Prayer	
Relaxation	
Relax Into Greatness	
Slower Breathing & Asana	
Massage	
Reflection	

The Four Desires Workbook

Choose one to three techniques from the list below to increase *vairagya* on a spiritual level:

Technique	Describe how you will apply 1-3 of the following techniques over the next 40 days.
Prayer	
Devotion	
Meditation	
Other	

"There are two pains in life: the pain of discipline and the pain of regret. We each choose which of the two we will suffer." – Anonymous

> *Throughout The Four Desires, I have asked you to do certain exercises and practices to help you improve the quality of your life: Did you do all of them? Did you do some of them? Did you do any of them? How completely have you embraced Adjustment? How much are you going to adjust after you've finished reading the book and doing the exercises?*

!Read pages 273-282 in *The Four Desires* about two principles that help illuminate the ideal approach to living: Adjustment and Contentment.

What is greater, the pain of you not having what you want or the pain of you making the changes necessary to getting it? Which ever one you believe is a greater source of pain, will determine your behavior, moreover your future.

You've come to the end of the book, the exercises and this workbook. The biggest factor in determining whether you will achieve your desires is you, or more specifically, the actions you do or do not take. What will inspire you enough to change and to do what is necessary to achieve or to become what you want? Ironically, often it's the pain of coming face-to-face with not achieving your goal. The pain of not doing, not honoring your soul's call, may well exceed all other pain.

It's time for you to turn your attention to the consequences of not following through and doing what you need to do to fulfill your destiny. Isn't it time you stop postponing your happiness?

!First, take a few minutes to read 283-289 about the pain of not changing, then complete the exercise below.

Time 10 minutes

Know the Consequences. On the following page, write about the consequences of your desire not being fulfilled. Include all the pain including emotional, financial, physical and spiritual. Identify the cost of not following through, of not taking the actions that move you toward achieving the life you want.

What is the specific impact on you and on your life if you do not make the necessary changes or if you fail to apply or continue applying any of the specific steps in *The Four Desires*?

"We are always being led by something.
However, only one thing can lead us to the ultimate freedom." – Rod Stryker

This final exercise is vital and a key part of *The Four Desires* process.

According to an ancient scripture, the "White Horse" is the Source of Life; it is also the light that dwells in your heart; it is your soul or essence. The message of this scripture is that you must nurture your relationship to the White Horse, and thus allow it to become the guiding force throughout your life.

Please read the piece on Contentment, including Shelly's story on pages 294-296 of *The Four Desires* as an example of the power of meditation to develop guidance and contentment. Then read The White Horse on pages 297-299.

When you finish reading these two excerpts from *The Four Desires,* get still and drop into effortless awareness for a few moments to cultivate contentment. What do you see, hear, feel and experience when you rest in complete contentment? In the space provided below, use any method you want to depict the feeling of contentment. You can write a poem, draw symbols or shapes, use colors, paste pictures and graphics or sketch drawings that depict contentment. You may even go back and reconnect with the scene you drew on pages 57-58 in the Create your Vision exercise. Keep it simple. Be authentic. Convey only what is revealed to you through this silence and reverence.

> ***"The more you insist on improving who and what you are,***
> ***the more you become master of your destiny." – Rod Stryker***

The Sanskrit term for practice is *abhyasa,* which means the sustained effort to be "there." Practice entails being mindful of the goal, while consistently endeavoring to reach it. For a practice to be effective, it must have 3 essential elements:

- ❖ It must be done for a long time
- ❖ It must be done consistently
- ❖ It must be done with love or reverence

! Read Establishing Your Practice on page 304-306 in *The Four Desires* about developing a consistent meditation practice, it's power to increase self-awareness and cultivate inner wisdom to lead you to who and what you are meant to be.

! Remember to practice the exercises in *The Four Desires* anytime you seek to find purpose, happiness, prosperity and freedom in your life.

! *The Four Desires* **Weekly Check-In**
Use the following page once a week for the next 6 months and as often as you want after that. It is important that you keep this weekly check-in going to stay on the right side of the Creation Equation.

---

*This is invaluable. I ask even my most senior students to continue to fill this form out on a weekly basis, long after they have completed the process of The Four Desires. There is no better way to see, with your own eyes, whether or not you are practicing The Four Desires and thus, serving your highest best interests.

After reading *The Four Desires and doing all the exercises*, complete this form weekly for the next 6 months. In order to establish a new and lasting momentum, check in with yourself often to continue creating a life of purpose, happiness, prosperity and freedom. Choose a day and time each week to set aside for this. Mark it on your calendar and make it part of your weekly routine if you truly want to move toward achievement of freedom and fulfillment.

Date: _____

What is your Dharma Code?

What is your *vikalpa?*

What is your *sankalpa*?

What is your Departure Point?

Which side of your creation equation is winning this week? Describe why.

Write down how many times this week you did the following:

Asana_____. Describe your practice and reflections:

Pranayama_____. Describe your practice and reflections:

Meditation_____average length of time _____. Describe your practice and reflections:

Yoga Nidra with *sankalpa* _____   *Dhi* Exercise _____

Departure Point/Seeding the Gap avg. # times per day _____. Reflections:

Conclusion

Going through the process of *The Four Desires* for the first time is just the beginning, you can repeat it as often as you'd like. You may want to select just one exercise to focus on or do several of them. You can complete the entire process from beginning to end again and again. Please, just practice. Consistently devote time to silence. The more you become established in this stillness, the more you will trust that Providence will provide you with everything you need, including guidance and wisdom.

> *Here are other recommendations to help guide you as you continue the process of The Four Desires. I have listed them in the order of importance, starting with the ones that I think will be the most helpful for you to do consistently. Don't over commit, choose just 2-3 and make a concerted effort to do them on a regular basis.*

1. Meditate daily. Choose any of the meditations from *The Four Desires*. Even if it's just 15 minutes, incorporate it into your routine just like brushing your teeth.
2. Practice Seeding the Gap everyday until you are in the momentum of living your DC and then use it with your *sankalpa*. Once you've accomplished your *sankalpa*, then, do the exercises again to create a new *sankalpa*.
3. Fill out *The Four Desires* Weekly Check-In.
4. Practice Relax Into Greatness at least three times a week.
5. Plan a yoga practice in your day that includes asana, pranayama and meditation.
6. Do a 40-day *vairagya* practice; use the practice log on pages 103 & 104 of this workbook.
7. Practice listening to and trusting your *dhi.*
8. Do daily check-ins with yourself, using the Daily Dhi Mind Map on page 102 of this workbook.
9. Redo your Know the Consequences exercises, on page 88 & 89 of this workbook.
10. Practice the Hidden Resistance Exercise anytime you feel stuck, to identify what's in the way of accomplishing your desires.
11. Post your DC in a place you will often see it: Mirror, refrigerator, car console, etc…
12. Take inventory of which exercises from this process you've completed, repeated, and when. There's a log on page 105.

Finally, if you have not yet, I strongly suggest joining a Four Desires Workshop with me or a Four Desires certified trainer. You can find where & when the trainings are held at **parayoga.com**.

Examples for Dharma Code

❖ I create and share from a place of fullness and power. I provide the deep nourishment my thriving requires. I fiercely commit to self-mastery.

❖ I stand confidently in the Spotlight.
I Create and Share Beauty
I trust and accept true love.
I vanquish dysfunction.

❖ I shine with my power and strength. I live for authenticity. I play effortlessly.

❖ I choose: Freedom... Love... and to be seen
I nourish myself and savor the beauty of life.
I Surrender trustfully, thus I am embraced by God.

❖ I vanquish dysfunction.
I trust and accept true love.
I stand confidently in the Spotlight, creating and sharing Beauty

❖ I courageously shine to lead a transformative life of empowerment, health, and sweet faith. I love my process—actively. I'm deeply connected and powerfully alive.

❖ I fearlessly embrace my power.
I breathe faith and self-acceptance into my life.
I receive and radiate love and vitality.
I abide in my inner abode of rest, steadiness, inner strength and calm.

❖ I create and share from my fullness and power. I provide the deep nourishment my thriving requires. I fiercely commit to self-mastery.

❖ I give form to my dreams. I love and create fearlessly.
I consistently nourish my mind, body and spirit.
I playfully rejoice in the present moment.

❖ I unconditionally trust that the universe and God are constantly supporting me.
I fearlessly choose enormity and self-care, creating countless opportunities for more joy.
I actively reach out to co-create magnificence with God, blind to other's perception of me.
I rest on this heavenly Divine throne, the master of my destiny.

III. Your *Vikalpa* Must:

1. Not be a label. A *vikalpa* is *not* descriptive of you or your life. A *vikalpa* is a *vasana,* which means it is a **desire**. Thus, to identify your *vikalpa,* you must state it in the form of an, "I want…" statement. *There are a few viable alternatives to this approach, I am afraid.* In short, this is most direct, if not, only approach, to uncovering your Deepest Driving Desire, the one that is creating your less than ideal destiny.

2. Begin your *vikalpa* with the words: "I want…." This acknowledges the fact that one, desire is the source of all of your actions, speech and thoughts and two, that even your destructive desires provide you with some pay off. To break free of the outcome they create, you must specify it as a desire—*it's that simple and that critical*—only then (with your inner desires out in the open) can you be free to live in line with your DC and achieve your *sankalpas.* Remember, Sarah's *vikalpa,* "At all costs, I want to avoid being hurt by someone I love." And Evan's *vikalpa,* "I want to avenge my father by having him see me die." Both are in direct opposition to their *sankalpas* and are making their lives more painful and their *sankalpas* all but impossible to fulfill, yet both are getting something (avoiding being hurt, revenge) from their holding onto their desires.

As you read through the examples of *vikalpa*s below, note that almost all of them needed to be refined. Initially, most made the mistake of wrongly identifying what they wanted. As I've said before, no one consciously wants to suffer. But we do want to avoid pain, uncomfortable feelings, disappointing parents or, we do want safety, maintaining the status quo, etc…. These desires are our priority—our Deepest Driving Desire, if you will. Since this is what we actually want, this is how your *vikalpa* must begin. Once you identified what you actually want, then the *vikalpa* goes on to recognize how or why. This should be clear in the examples below:

***VIKALPA* EXAMPLES:**

Original	*Changed to:*
❖ I want to be angry and victimized to remain anonymous.	❖ I want to remain anonymous, so I stay angry and victimized.
❖ I want to avoid expressing myself fully because I am afraid of being judged, hurt and rejected by others.	❖ I want to avoid being judged, hurt and rejected by others, so I avoid expressing myself fully.
❖ I want to let others make my decisions for me, because if they don't work out, I'm not to blame.	❖ I want to avoid the shame of making mistakes and choosing wrongly, so I let others make my decisions for me… and then blame them for what's wrong with my life.

Guidelines & Examples for Vikalpa

Original	*Changed to:*
❖ I want to be an unlovable drudge, ignoring my body and soul, chained to a job no better than my parents'	❖ I want to avoid surpassing my parents, so I chain myself to drudgery, lovelessness and a job that ignores my body and soul.
❖ I want to avoid sharing my gifts so that my worst fear of having nothing special to offer in this world is not confirmed.	❖ I want to avoid confirming my worst fear—that I have nothing special to offer the world—so I neglect my gifts and choose not to share them.
❖ I want to fail so that I can stay comfortable in the certainty that I will never be happy, safe or successful.	❖ I want to stay comfortable (in the certainty that I will never be happy, safe or successful) so, I seek out and create failure.
❖ I want to be alone with my books & my imagination, because every time I connect with others I let them down.	❖ I want to avoid letting others down so, I stay alone with my books and imagination.
❖ I want to take care of others so I avoid taking care of myself.	❖ I want to avoid taking care of myself, so I take care of others.
❖ I want to be loved and admired by EVERYBODY, no matter the toll it takes and on my body, mind and soul.	*(Didn't need to be changed)*
❖ I want to avoid ever being hurt again so, I create an impenetrable emotional wall around myself.	*(Didn't need to be changed)*

Examples of Dharma Code Curing Vikalpas

Original DC	Vikalpa	Final Revised DC
Radiant, strong and expansive, my Goddess-like being loves, serves and gives.	I want to avenge my parents and ex-husband because of their lack of love and support—by excelling at all costs—working, giving and taking care of everyone else, and thus getting sicker and sicker.	I choose freedom, thus I thrive. I choose to be seen, thus I am loved. I choose self-nourishment, thus I savor the beauty of life. I choose trustful Surrender, thus I am embraced by God and Goddess
I fearlessly share my magnitude with the world	I want to avoid answering the call of my own heart, dimming it's bright light—so I can protect my father, and prove him right, that, "I will never amount to anything."	I unshackle myself from the past. I, no one else, define who I am. I effortlessly create beauty wherever I go, undistracted by others' success. I act, think and feel as Radiance acts, thinks and feels.
I gracefully radiate strength and fearlessness that inspires and empowers myself and others. I light fires!	I want to avoid confirming my worst fear—that I have nothing special to offer the world—so I neglect my gifts and choose not to share them.	I breathe faith and self-acceptance into my life. I fearlessly embrace my power. I receive and radiate love and vitality. My soul soars, fulfilling its unique and sacred duty. I rest in steady inner strength and calm.
Standing confidently in the Spotlight, I create and Share Beauty	1. I want to avoid standing out/being in the spotlight of the artist, to drown out fear, vulnerability and the possibility of being taken seriously, so I submerge, distract, avoid my powerful voice and presence. 2. I want the security of the familiar, by continuing to feed my dysfunctional untrusting, unloving & inauthentic relationship to my mother	I stand confidently in the Spotlight. I Create and Share Beauty I trust and accept true love. I vanquish dysfunction.

II. Your *Sankalpa* Must:

1. READ LIKE FACT. Remember that the most effective way to craft the language of your *sankalpa* is to feel and recognize the benefits of having already achieved it. The "new-age" approach is to imagine you tell someone, who cares about you, the facts about why you are so thrilled and fulfilled. If it doesn't read like something you would say, it needs rewriting. Or if you prefer you can state it as "I can, I will, I must..." statements.

2. BE WRITTEN IN PRESENT OR PERHAPS PAST TENSE. Consider the inclusion of emotional language that describes the feelings you associate with it having already come to fruition.

3. BE SPECIFIC. It is important that you can clearly judge whether or not you have achieved it. *Sankalpas* that have no end point or are overtly qualitative are not *sankalpas*.

4. ADDRESS AT LEAST ONE OF THE FOUR DESIRES, otherwise it is likely that your *sankalpa* is more of a DC.

5. BE ACHIEVABLE IN SIX TO EIGHTEEN MONTHS. Remember that at least 51% of you must believe that it is achievable — more belief is better.

6. TOUCH YOUR CORE. It should elicit a visceral response when you say or think of it.

7. BE CLEAR AND SHORT ENOUGH TO REMEMBER. When you repeat your *sankalpa* either out loud or silently, it should be the same statement(s). Make it clear so you can remember it precisely. No more than 4 or 5 sentences at most.

8. HAVE AN ACCOMPANYING IMAGE AND FEELING. Recall the process of writing the paragraph that led you to it. Visualization and emotion is an essential part of the exercise and how you came to your *sankalpa*. It's also essential to achieving it.

***SANKALPA* EXAMPLES:**

NEW AGE APPROACH *SANKALPAS*

- ❖ I'm so excited! I just finished leading my first 8-week life enhancement series. My clients are feeling empowered and thriving, and I am feeling fulfilled and living my *dharma*.

- ❖ I have a loving partner; together we share and support each other and each other's lives.

- ❖ I have the rest and clarity I need to live in balance, because I meditate daily.

- ❖ The home remodel is complete! I have the stability and resources to deepen my practice.

- ❖ I am happy, fearless and in my power; I met my financial goal and increased my income by more than 50%.

- ❖ I can write and publish my first book by next fall.

  I must write and publish my first book by next fall.

  I will write and publish my first book by next fall.

- ❖ I can keep my weight below 133 pounds by eating foods that nourish me.

  I must keep my weight below 133 pounds by eating foods that nourish me.

  I will keep my weight below 133 pounds by eating foods that nourish me.

- ❖ I can double the revenue of my new business, and create a viable, sought after yoga media and lifestyle brand steeped in tradition.

  I must double the revenue of my new business, and create a viable, sought after yoga media and lifestyle brand steeped in tradition.

  I will double the revenue of my new business, and create a viable, sought after yoga media and lifestyle brand steeped in tradition.

- ❖ I can commit to and work on my marriage to help us find peace, love, forgiveness and mutual respect.

  I must commit to and work on my marriage to help us find peace, love, forgiveness and mutual respect.

  I will commit to and work on my marriage to help us find peace, love, forgiveness and mutual respect.

Daily Dhi Mind Map

Complete a daily mind map. After practicing meditation to still your mind (feel free to use any from the companion CD) and applying the technique to access your *dhi* from page 204 in *The Four Desires*, use the mind map below to write your specific question for Dhi inside the oval. As you still the mind and access *dhi,* write what you hear on spokes that you draw around each circle.

Below is a basic model of what a daily mind map may look like. Create your own in a journal. Sketch in and fill out spokes around each circle spontaneously, in whatever order ideas occur to you. Feel free to change the title in any or all of the circles. Write today's "Question for *dhi*" in the circle, then pause and quietly write down what you hear from your intuition, *dhi*. Remember: draw one line at a time and fill it in before creating a new line.

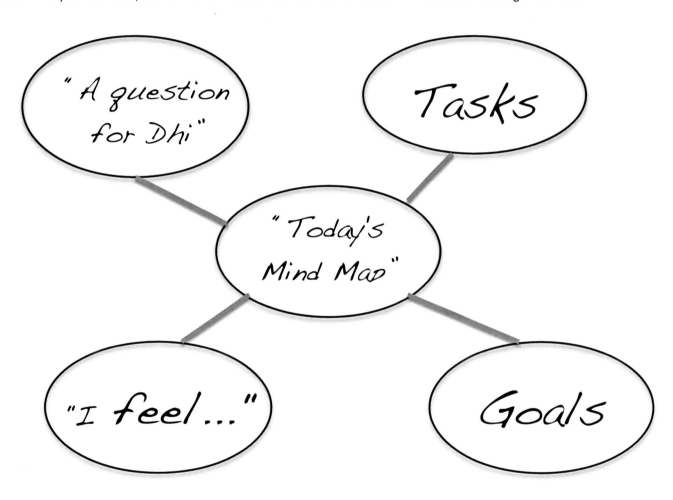

40-Day Vairagya Practice Log

Self Reflection: Place a check mark beside the practices you incorporated into your day:

Day	1	2	3	4	5	6	7	8	9	10	11	12	13	14	15	16	17	18	19	20
External																				
Compromise																				
Selfless Service																				
Charity																				
Humility																				
Compassion																				
Forgiveness																				
Internal																				
Meditation																				
Prayer																				
Relaxation																				
Relax Into Greatness																				
Slower Breathing																				
Asana																				
Massage																				
Reflection																				
Spiritual																				
Prayer																				
Devotion																				
Meditation																				

Commit to reflecting for 5 minutes a day for the next 40 days. Make time at some point toward the end of your day to do this quick self check-in. Plan to do it for the next 40 days consistently.

40-Day Vairagya Practice Log

Self Reflection: Place a check mark beside the practices you incorporated into your day:

Day	21	22	23	24	25	26	27	28	29	30	31	32	33	34	35	36	37	38	39	40
External																				
Compromise																				
Selfless Service																				
Charity																				
Humility																				
Compassion																				
Forgiveness																				
Internal																				
Meditation																				
Prayer																				
Relaxation																				
Relax Into Greatness																				
Slower Breathing																				
Asana																				
Massage																				
Reflection																				
Spiritual																				
Prayer																				
Devotion																				
Meditation																				

Commit to reflecting for 5 minutes a day for the next 40 days. Make time at some point toward the end of your day to do this quick self check-in. Plan to do it for the next 40 days consistently.

The Four Desires Exercise Log

EXERCISE	TFD PAGE	WKBK PAGE	DATE COMPLETED/REPEATED
Uncover Your Mighty Purpose			
Thriving Moment Poem		4-5	
Testimonial Exercise, The	51	6-16	
1st Draft of Your Dharma Code		17-18 26-30	
An Experiment in Watching Your Mind Think	68	19	
Meditation on The Breath	72, companion CD	20	
Three Words		21	
Themes in Your Life		22-24	
Capturing the Essentials		25	
2nd Draft of The Dharma Code		47-52	
Dharma Code Checklist		53	
Achieve Something Great			
Sankalpa Exercise, The	42-45, 64-66, 97	31-34, 54-56	
Bliss Meditation, The	99, companion CD	33	
Create Your Vision		57-58	
1st Draft of Your Sankalpa	106	59-60	
Sankalpa 2.0		61	
What is Keeping You From Greatness			
Your Vikalpa(s)	146	35-46	
Master Your Destiny			
Creation Equation, The	119	62	
Meditation to Increase Shakti	134, companion CD	63	
Goodbye Resistance	152-153	64-65	
List Your Habits	154	66-67	
Relax Into Greatness	166, companion CD	68	
Hidden Resistance Exercise, The	172	69-70	
Create Your Departure Point, Then Seed The Gap	179	71-72	
Get in the Present		73	
Healing The Heart Meditation	202, companion CD	74	
Access Your Intuition	204	75	
48 Hours Of Fearless Action	220	76-77	
Vairagya Exercise Pt. I, The	235	78-79	
Vairagya Exercise Pt. II, The	241	80-81	

How to Increase Vairagya	251	82	
Let Go: Meditation to Increase Vairagya	258, companion CD	83	
Plan to Increase Vairagya		84-86	
Pain of Not Changing, The	288	87-88	
White Horse, The	297	89-90	
The Practice		91	
Four Desires Check-In, The		92	
References and Extras To Help You Master Your Destiny			
Examples for Dharma Code		94	
Guidelines & Examples for Vikalpa		95-96	
Examples of Dharma Code Curing Vikalpa		97	
Guidelines & Examples for Sankalpa		98-99	
Daily Dhi Mind Map		100	
40-Day Vairagya Practice Log		101-102	
Stories		105	
The Four Desires Index		106-111	

Stories

The Four Desires Index

The Four Desires Workbook

Y
Yajur Veda, 7
Yoga, xiii,
Yoga Nidra, 161, 162, 163
Yoga Sutras, 225